How to Get Your Customers Swearing by You, Not at You

Telephone Doctor's Guide to Customer Service Training

Nancy Friedman
The Telephone Doctor®

HRD Press • Amherst • Massachusetts

Published by: HRD Press, Inc.
22 Amherst Road
Amherst, MA 01002
1-800-822-2801 (U.S. and Canada)
413-253-3488
413-253-3490 (fax)
www.hrdpress.com

ISBN 978-1-59996-151-4

Cover design by Eileen Klockars
Editorial services by Mary Anne Brooks, FAB50 Marketing, and
Sally Farnham
Production services by Anctil Virtual Office

*This book is dedicated to my mother, Esther Mollner,
who told me years ago,
"Nancy, there's very little new . . . just new people
doing it. . . ."*

Mom . . . you were right! Thanks. I miss you very much.

Your loving daughter,
Nancy

Contents

Acknowledgments

Dr. Ernie Tompkins—Tompkins Consulting, Winston Salem, NC

Valerie K. Phillips—Executive Assistant to Nancy J. Friedman, St. Louis, MO

Nancie O'Neille—Pinnacle Entertainment, Las Vegas, NV

Tom Hopkins—Tom Hopkins International, Scottsdale, AZ

Jack Falvey—MakingTheNumbers.com, Londonderry, NH

Charles Graves—Gale, a part of Cengage Learning, Farmington Hills, MI

Charlie Wallace—Executive Director, Quality Service Contractors (QSC), Falls Church, VA

Kelly Luvison—Executive Vice President, GateHouse Media, Inc., Fairport, NY

Mary Anne Brooks—FAB50 Marketing/Basic Business Solutions, St. Louis, MO

My children—David Friedman and Linda Steinberg

My husband—Dick Friedman

All my friends at Telephone Doctor Customer Service Training

All my friends at Weatherline Inc.

Why This Book Is Important to You

"Let's do some customer service training," says the boss.

That's great you think. But, where do I start?

There are so many folks who want to do customer service training and have no idea *where* to start. Nancy's message gets you off on the right foot and keeps you there.

This book is designed to make it easy for you—whether you're a novice at the customer service game or the most experienced facilitator.

In the Beginning: The Story

"Your People Stink!"

Since 1983, Telephone Doctor® Inc. has provided training in customer service and telephone skills.

Its beginning, rather curiously, was a result of my dissatisfaction with the insurance agent we were using for my husband's first business, Weatherline Inc. Frustrated with his agency's lack of service and continually being told what they "couldn't do" and what I "had to do," I was fed up with this type of "service." So I called him one day to cancel all our policies. This was no small job: we were one of his largest accounts. He asked why we were canceling, and I told him rather directly, "Your people stink!" I told him that his people were abrupt, unhelpful, unfriendly, and even outright rude at times. I didn't need to be treated like that anymore. I wouldn't be treated like that anymore!

He told me, "You know, Nancy, you're right. When I call your office, I'm treated like a king, and I'm not even a customer."

"Michael," I told him, "we treat our wrong numbers better than you treat your customers!"

He asked me if I'd do him a favor and come to his office and show his people how they should treat customers.

I went to his office out of love. Michael told his staff of a dozen or so that I was coming in "to talk to them." Since I didn't have a written presentation, I talked to them from the heart. I told them, "At our office, we say 'please,' 'thank you,' 'you're welcome,' and 'have a nice weekend.' At our office we make sure we're in a good mood when we talk to customers." I told them how I wanted to be treated. It seemed like good old common sense to me.

And would you believe it? The people couldn't write down my information fast enough.

I don't think I spoke more than 15 minutes. As I was leaving, the president of the agency stopped me because he wanted to thank me. "We really learned some new things today!" he said.

That evening, over dinner, I told my husband, Dick, about what had happened that day—about calling the agency, being asked to come over to talk to the staff, being thanked by the president of the agency—all for things that my husband and I feel are instinctual, such as breathing in and breathing out.

In my husband's infinite wisdom, he told me, "Don't ever be surprised, Nancy. No one has ever shown them."

Shortly thereafter, I was visiting with one of our Weatherline clients, the general manager of a midwestern city's newspaper. In casual conversation, I told him about my call to the insurance agency and what the president of the agency told me. The very next day, the same manager called me. Based on what we had talked about, he wanted me to come to his paper and train his people. He informed me he had 300 employees. "When can you come and talk to us?" he asked. As soon as I write the program, I thought to myself.

Well I burned the midnight oil and wrote a four-hour program on customer service and telephone skills. I wrote from the heart about the things I had learned over the years—things that my mother and father taught me. It took me a few late nights, but finally, after a few weeks, I completed what I felt was a strong presentation—information that would help them increase profits and gain a competitive edge.

I made arrangements with the newspaper and flew to Davenport, Iowa, and delivered four 4-hour programs. The first program was presented only to managers, because the general manager said to me, "If the program is to work—and I want it to—it must start at the top, Nancy. It must dribble down. It cannot dribble up."

At the end of the first program, the editor of the newspaper came over to me and said, "You're very good, Nancy. You sure have all the cures. I'm gonna call you the doctor— you're the Telephone Doctor!"

And that's how the Telephone Doctor® was born.

Telephone Doctor® started by providing seminars to corporations and associations all over the country. This book has been written, in part, for the hundreds of smaller staffed offices that have asked me for an answer to their customer service training. I often hear, "Nancy, how can we do this ourselves?"

Eventually we started presenting our programs to larger companies: Fortune 500 companies. They, too, wanted to know *how* they could design a customer service training program for their company that would resemble ours. *How to Get Your Customers Swearing by You, Not at You: Telephone Doctor's Guide to Customer Service Training* will make it easy and fun for anyone who wants to put customer service training into place at his or her company. It's not rocket science, it's not brain surgery, but it does require time and a commitment to make it right.

After the seminars became successful, clients started asking us for follow-up. They told us our programs were wonderful, but they asked questions such as what happens in about three to six months when the attendees start forgetting? Or worse, slipping back into old habits? And, what about new employees? What would they do if management wasn't available? Clients wanted a program for follow-up.

Odd as it seems now, in the beginning, I was afraid to put our material on electronic media. I knew our material was original, and I feared it would be copied. There were, however, enough determined and convincing clients who succeeded in talking my husband and me into writing a video program. We called it simply *On Incoming Calls*. We took five points from our seminar that we felt would help the clients during follow-up and would also be a great refresher course for new and longtime employees.

The program did quite well, and we were very pleased. We saw that it stood alone as its own training device. The facilitator's guide that we had prepared with it made the program very easy to deliver. We even included some desktop reminder cards for employees who saw the presentation.

About a year later, one of our faithful Telephone Doctor® clients called to ask when our second program would be available. "Second program?" my husband and I asked in unison. "Yes," they said, "you need a sequel." Well, always ones to make clients happy, Dick and I put pen to paper and came up with yet a second program and aptly named it *More on Incoming Calls*.

In the meantime, we upgraded our seminars and put some of the techniques that were in the seminar into the second program so that clients could use it as follow-up to ensure continued good customer service.

Fast forward to the 21st century: Telephone Doctor® now has a library of programs consisting of 16 modules, with over 100 customer service techniques. We have DVDs, audios, books, and other related training materials.

Over the years, speaking at conferences and organizations around the country, I've learned many things. One of the most interesting things is when I ask attendees how many of them have had some sort of new employee orientation on customer service. You'd be amazed how few of them have ever had training in this vital area.

You know, nobody hires bad people. No one runs an ad saying, "Wanted: rude, depressed individuals needed to insult our customers." On the contrary, companies hire potentially good people, but untrained people—people untrained in the area of customer service.

And that, quite simply, is the underlying philosophy of the Telephone Doctor® in all its training endeavors:

> Develop programs of common-sense training (and retraining) to achieve an ever-improving degree of excellence in customer service!

Now your organization, large or small, can do the same with *How to Get Your Customers Swearing by You, Not at You: Telephone Doctor's Guide to Customer Service Training.* Enjoy!

Fondly,

Nancy J. Friedman
The Telephone Doctor

How to Use This Book: Honestly, It's Easy!

You're working very diligently when one day the boss comes up and says, "We need to improve our customer service. We've got to train our people. . . ."

As we all know, in boss- or manager-ese talk, the operative word "we" means "you"!

Yes, *you*! Now *you've* got to develop customer service training for your company or department. Congratulations! Where do you start?

Don't move. You're in the right place. *How to Get Your Customers Swearing by You, Not at You: Telephone Doctor's Guide to Customer Service Training* is geared to those who are faced with the challenge of developing effective customer service training.

Whether you're a professional facilitator in the workplace or a small business owner, you or your company work very hard to make sure your customers are treated well. You work hard to be sure you *keep* your customers. And yet, one day you lose a customer, all because someone didn't say or do the right thing for them. If this scenario has occurred at your organization, you'll find *How to Get Your Customers Swearing by You, Not at You: Telephone Doctor's Guide to Customer Service Training* an invaluable resource of customer service material, tips, and ideas.

While poor customer service is certainly a serious subject and needs to be improved, you'll find some tips and ideas presented in a lighthearted manner. There is no reason learning it should be dreary and unexciting. It should be fun to teach and learn. It should be presented and accepted enthusiastically.

At the conclusion of my Telephone Doctor® presentations, someone invariably comes up to me and says, "Nancy, the information you gave was super. I loved what you said, but how do I make a customer service training program for my people? What's the first step?" I never had a formal answer for those individuals. Now I do, and I'll share them with you.

KEY POINT: *How to Get Your Customers Swearing by You, Not at You: Telephone Doctor's Guide to Customer Service Training* is readable and the suggestions are easily adaptable.

If I had only a few minutes of your time, I would explain putting a customer service training program together like this:

- Find out what your customers like and don't like. Talk to your customers and your employees.

- From the information you gather, decide what topics you'll teach your employees to let them know what they need to do in order to provide what the customers want.

- Share with your employees the customer comments you've collected in the best possible way you can.

- Be sure what you taught them works!

That's the basic information within *How to Get Your Customers Swearing by You, Not at You: Telephone Doctor's Guide to Customer Service Training*. We have put the above information in an easy-to-read, fun-to-use format.

Here are the "how-to" components that will guide you through the four steps in the essential process of developing a customer service training program:

1. **Analysis:**   Find out what customers like and don't like.
2. **Design:**   What topics should you talk about?
3. **Delivery:**   How should you deliver the topic information?
4. **Evaluation:** How did it go?

I've added one more step:

5. **Other Considerations**

Plus, there are shorter commentaries on aspects of training and customer service that may provide new and fresh insights into the subject. Browse through them as you develop your program, and see if they don't help to put new touches on the subject! Look at the process in a new light.

So when the boss says, "*We* should do something about customer service training," you will be ready to reply, "Sure, no problem!"

And, again, in developing your own customer service training program, be sure to have some fun!

How do you use this book to develop your own customer service program? Look at our diagram on the following page, see what you need to do first, and proceed. It's easy!

Components

ANALYSIS

Analysis: What Is It?

KISS
Audience
Job Knowledge
Barriers to Training
Management Involvement

DESIGN

Design: Not as Scary as It Sounds

Content   Housekeeping
Budget & Costs   Facilitator's
EDPF   Guides
Getting Started   Workbooks
Resources   Role Playing
Icebreakers   Copyright

DELIVERY

Delivery: The Fun Part

Selling the Training to the
    Attendees
Lecturing
Questions
Problem Attendees
Rewards
Finishing with a Flourish

EVALUATION

Evaluation: How'd Ya Do?

Classroom Evaluations
Testing
Behavior Change
Why Your Training Didn't Work

OTHER CONSIDERATIONS

It Should Never Take Two People to Deliver Good Customer Service
Us in Customer   Band-Aid Training   Potpourri
Customer Service Training Topics

Analysis
Component

Analysis: What Is It?

Analysis, or needs assessment, is finding out what your customers like and don't like about how you treat them. Assessment of needs is the first component of four in the formal development of a customer service training program.

An informal method of assessing needs would be to call your office and ask for yourself, a service, or a product. You'll determine within minutes if your staff needs customer service training. If your company is in the retail industry, consider doing a "mystery shopper" experience: have a friend or coworker walk into a location and ask for something. Get his reaction on how he was treated. It's easier than you think. What you may want to assess further is *what* part of customer service training is needed and *who* needs the training. That's an important part of the needs assessment. But you should go in with the belief that the need is already there.

This method of assessing needs is usually quick, direct, and accurate. However, a more structured, formal approach can be used in addition to any observations made above.

When you want to initiate customer service training, you need to understand the current status of your organization's customer service. Learning as much as possible about the current situation is the first step in creating a customer service training program.

Step 1: Questions, Questions, Questions

In initiating your program, begin by asking questions and monitoring employee performance. This way you determine the quality level of customer service currently being provided by your organization.

Analysis, or needs assessment, determines the "gap" between where you are as an organization (or department) regarding customer service and where you want to be. This requires not only an assessment of *what is,* but also a determination of *what should be.* Contrast the level of performance with the level of quality that is expected. Look for flaws between what *is* being done and what *should* be done and fill in the gaps— that's the customer service training you're looking for.

EXAMPLE: You want your employees to make sure every contact with a customer includes a simple "please" and "thank you." Your analysis data (however you may have done it) shows they are not doing this. Thus you're looking for customer service training that will teach your employees to say "please" and "thank you."

While this analogy is a basic, common-sense example, it's frightening how many employees don't use those words in their contact with customers.

You also want to identify things you do well as an
organization and some of the specific people who do it well.
This gives you some of the good things you already do as a
benchmark to build on, such as:

> "When we handle 'X' type of complaints,
> we're always very good at (fill in)."

In identifying some of the individuals who perform their jobs
well, you are creating your own database of resource people
who can become content help for you when you get into the
content portion of customer service training.

EXAMPLE: If someone does really well in handling difficult
customers, irate customers, and such, you'll want
to pay particular attention to how he or she does
it and let that person become your *content* expert
on that topic. They can also become a mentor for
individuals needing specific help.

Step 2: The Tools

Some of the tools used for this analysis can be interviews with **focus groups.** These groups should consist of your customers who will be available for you to ask questions about how they are treated on a continuous basis, and most importantly, how they want to be treated.

They shouldn't be afraid to voice what they like about your company and what they don't like. Focus groups, while usually small in size (normally 10 to 12 people), can be a powerful part of your analysis. It's like having an outside board member: they tell it like it is.

Pencil/paper surveys, questionnaires, or any other comment forms will help you get to know your customers.

Telephone surveys are not my favorite tool. It seems that customers don't mind filling out a form or talking face-to-face (or frequently now by e-mail), but for whatever reason, telephone surveys are still thought of as telemarketing. Research-wise, telephone surveys don't seem to get as good a response or results as we would want in the end. Even though you may hire an outside company to do the telephone survey, it is still perceived as telemarketing by the customer. There are, of course, very reputable companies that can handle a phone survey well and provide you the information needed to determine what the customer wants.

For the best results, whatever method you use, **make it easy for the customer.** Make it easy for them to talk with you, and make it easy for them to fill out any forms. The customer shouldn't need to spend more than 10 or 15 minutes to give you the information needed.

Be sure to include three groups of people in your analysis: (1) your customers, (2) your employees, and (3) top management.

KEY POINT: Whichever method you use, how you conduct the survey to get the information you need is not nearly as important as the fact that you do it.

Group 1: Your Customers

What do customers say you do well? What are the things that they're disappointed with and don't like, in terms of how they are treated? Reach out and talk with your customers in many ways. Be sure to let them know how the data will be used.

Also, be certain the customers you question give information based on their own experience with your company. If the person you are surveying has never called your company, it wouldn't make much sense to ask how he or she felt that he or she was treated during the call. You need to do "apple-to-apple" comparisons in your analysis.

EXAMPLE: If you want to know how your customers are relating to the way they're first treated when they walk into your store, then "catch them in the act," if you will. In other words, have your surveyor talk with customers as they are leaving the store—while the experience is still fresh.

A simple way to get a customer's attention might be "Would you have a quick moment to help us with our customer service survey?" Again, make it easy for the customer. This opportunity is a great way to make sure your customer service is starting out on the right foot. Just marching up to someone as they're leaving your store and stating you want to "talk with them" is not good customer service. Practice how you'll get the attention of the customer, and then practice some more. This is one way the customer will judge your service. In the first 30 seconds of the interaction, your customer forms an opinion of the surveyor. Make sure it's a good one.

You also might consider offering the customer some sort of incentive.

EXAMPLE: I recently received a magazine survey telling me that if I took the time to fill it out, I would be eligible to receive one of five $100 gift certificates, and, in addition, if I were one of the first 100 respondents, I would get a sport shirt with the company logo.

Here was a company that offered me, the customer, something extra in exchange for taking the time to answer its survey questions.

There are other ways to offer customers something to make them feel their time for talking with someone or filling out a form is valuable. A small but nice reward for the customer is a good idea.

Be sure customers know the information will be kept confidential. You don't need to be too concerned about getting their names. While that might be nice, it's not nearly as important as the information the customer will share with you.

Group 2: Your Employees

What are the things employees think they do well as they relate to customers? What are the things they feel they do not do as well? Or what are the things they are not as clear on as to how they should react or respond?

Again, how you get this information is critical. It's not always that employees don't want to give good customer service—they may not know how.

This is most often the case. You need to pay attention to this. If your customer service reps and front line employees seem wary of and withdrawn from this type of analysis or questioning, you can, of course, phrase the questions so that they describe what is right and what is done well.

EXAMPLE: "We have an opportunity to enhance policies and procedures. Your opinion is regarded as very important. Tell us how we can help you do a better job."

This "open arms" method will draw employees into the survey more easily. Again, you are looking for positive as well as negative feedback. Assure the employees the information they share with you is confidential and will in no way be used against them. This will help them open up.

 KEY POINT: It's not always that employees don't want to give good customer service—they may not know how.

Group 3: Top Management

The third group you want to hear from is the management group. Remember, they may be the ones who asked for customer service training.

Supervisors, department/division heads, and top management are essential to a comprehensive understanding of your training needs. It's very important to hear from all management levels, because it will give you a broader scope of what the needs are. One of the questions you need to ask top management is "What do you see your employees doing well in relation to customer service?"

And then the next questions to ask is "What are the things you think are not done as well, or what changes would you like to see as they relate to customer service?" This gives the group a chance to think from a broader base.

When you start analyzing their needs, you'll have a lot more information to assess. All of this information is related to your organization—from the people who know the most about it. And the best part? It's all yours.

Part of your analysis must include determining whether the employees know the procedures. Do they know what your customer service policies are? Do they know what your company's corporate policy is in terms of how to respond to certain types of complaints or difficult situations? Do they know where to go for a specific complaint?

EXAMPLE: You're a facilitator for a newspaper. One of the major complaints from your customers might be "I didn't get my paper today." What is the procedure for that? Does the employee know?

Another area to examine is when an employee knows what to do, but isn't doing it well. So in your analysis, you are looking for how much should be about *content* and how much should be about the actual *"how to"* (how to deliver positive customer service).

 KEY POINT: What do you see your employees doing well in relation to customer service?

Mission Statement

One of the key areas to include when assessing your customer service needs is your organization's mission statement—the values, purpose, and ideals of your company. This will help round out the customer service analysis.

What is your organization's mission statement? Don't panic if you don't have one—some companies don't. But if you do, be sure it is brought out in the hiring process. Let your prospective employees hear that information as soon as you can.

If you do have one, is it up to date? Where is your company's mission statement displayed? Is it on your desk? Or the wall? Can you find it quickly? Do all employees receive a copy of it in their new employee orientation package?

The analysis, or needs assessment, identifies both strengths and weaknesses in satisfying customers. This, therefore, will forecast a customer service training program that will match your needs.

Simply put, it's a matter of recognizing the status of customer service performance and then relating that to training opportunities.

It also is a good idea to do your analysis in stages and make it an ongoing process. Please don't perform a one-time analysis and think, "There, now I know what our customers want—and that's that."

The time and effort spent in reviewing customer contact with customer service representatives is typically believed to be the *most beneficial phase* of internal performance analysis.

The process of interviewing and questioning customer service personnel often can detect flaws in an organization that are extraneous to the customer service process itself.

The overriding service system may be flawed, the tools and technologies may require improvement, and goals and procedures may not be clearly defined.

These and a host of similar situations can be causes of customer service problems apart from poor performance by employees. These flaws may be identified in the analysis research and should be taken seriously as "internal customer comments."

 KEY POINT: Your company mission statement was designed for the company, not for the customer.

Next?

You've gotten information from your three groups: your customers, your employees, and your management group. You've asked the questions and compared apples to apples. You've collected the data and organized it. Now what?

Even if not mandatory, it would be desirable to submit a status or progress report to management of the results of the analysis process. Problems solvable by customer service training should be separated from those related to nontraining issues. These should be in the report to top management.

The customer accolades and criticisms directly relating to customer service should be compiled to provide an overview of the status of customer service in the organization. Objective answers such as "yes" and "no" or ratings from "1 to 5" can be totaled.

At the end of your analysis, include a section providing a sense of direction for improving customer service.

This first step, the analysis, represents the framework for the construction of the entire training program design.

Summary of Analysis

The analysis process is where you find out what your customers and employees think of how you treat them. Analyze what you have found out, and then *fix* it.

Sounds simple doesn't it? Well it is. Finding out what your customers think of you is not rocket science and should not be difficult. Keep your surveys simple, easy to fill out, and easy to analyze. You'll be able to fix the problem areas much quicker that way.

EXAMPLE: A while back, my husband and I went to one of those large stores that sell everything for a lot less than retail. After I wrote out my check at the counter, the clerk decided that the manager needed to get more information on our account. The manager came over, took the check, and was gone for about ten minutes. This kept the line from moving, and my husband and I were left wondering what the heck was going on.

After we questioned the clerk, who didn't know anything more than we did, the manager finally came back and said, "Okay, it's fine," and she started to leave without saying anything. I could have let her go, however, I felt we were due an explanation.

"Well," she said, "we needed more information on your account, and it was taking me longer than I thought." No apologies. No explanation of any sort.

First, before leaving with my check, the manager should have explained to me exactly where she was going and what she would be doing. It is poor customer service to leave a customer standing in a line for any length of time (and creating a longer line, at that) without some sort of clarification.

13

Second, the clerk should have been informed ahead of time about what occurs when a manager takes a check from a customer. The clerk should have been able to tell me what was going on with my check. That would be job knowledge. Instead, I got a blank stare and a big, "Gee, I don't know."

TELEPHONE DOCTOR® CUSTOMER SERVICE TIP:	Make it *easy* to do business with your company. The more forms you have people fill out or the more questions you ask without giving a reason are both ways for customers to not enjoy doing business with you.

KISS:
It's Not Rocket Science

Keep It Simple, Simon

Remember, customer service is not rocket science. It is common sense that, unfortunately, is not all that common these days.

In training *delivery,* be sure to explain customer service in plain, everyday language. This will help attendees understand and remember what you said. Words that make the employee stop and think, "I wonder what that means?" become ineffective in training. Again, keep it simple.

In training *evaluation,* some of the simplest, most straight-forward forms can provide valuable feedback on your class and suggest direction for the future.

Analysis of customer service needs can be simple, too. You probably already know some areas of excellence in your organization, as well as a gut feeling for where some areas for improvement are. Throughout analysis and design, make sure you keep it simple.

Audience:
Know Whom You're Training

Whom should you train on customer service? How do you decide whom to train? (I could make this chapter very short and simply say everyone!)

We've all heard that the first person who answers the phone or greets the customer is the most important person in the company to receive customer service training. That person represents the entire company, so start with the receptionists and front line people. Right? Well, that used to be right. However, today, with direct inward dial or voice mail, any employee can be the first person a customer talks with at your company. In many corporations, customers can call the president directly because they now answer their own phones. Therefore, no one should be exempt from customer service training.

TELEPHONE DOCTOR® CUSTOMER SERVICE TIP:	Whoever answers is the company.

What happens when someone is out the day of the customer service training? Or someone gets transferred into a department from an area where they didn't get the customer service training? What about new employees? What do those people tell the customer?

"Oh, gee. I'm very sorry. I was sick the day they did the customer service training and didn't get it—so you're stuck with me."

If you find yourself training only one department, it is pretty well guaranteed you'll be missing a lot of business. Certainly we need to increase the level and intensity of the Customer Service Department and Consumer Affairs people, but you know as well as I do that customers can and do come into any area and department of your company.

Let's go over a few ways to select the first group to receive training and then continue down the line.

First, get a list of all employees. If you're a small company, that's not going to be a big job. If you're a big company, it's probably already done for you. Check with your Human Resource or Personnel Department and ask for a list of those in your department and others if needed.

Once you have your list, be sure you understand what these employees do. Are they interacting with internal customers (individuals within your organization), external customers (individuals outside your organization), or both? Your internal customers are a critical part of customer service training.

After you have established your list of employees, what they do, and how they interact with your customers *and with each other,* it is a good idea to re-interview some of these employees. It's key to know your employees and how they feel about customers and their coworkers. Hearing how your employees feel about your customers will help you select what training resources you'll use. It will be very interesting. You might have people who think they don't interact with customers, even though they talk with them every day! Take the time to talk with your employees. Make a short list of questions to ask them.

Prepare a simple form for employees to fill out. A few sample questions could include the following:

- How many customer calls do you get on a daily basis?
- Do you receive more calls from inside the office or outside the office? (This will help you determine how much internal customer service they provide along with the external service.)

- What is the most common question, situation, or comment you get from a customer? Is it an internal or external customer?

- Do you receive the same question over and over, or are you challenged by different questions each time?

- Do you get irate callers?

- Are your calls technically oriented? Are the questions from within the company, from another employee, or from an outside customer?

- How often do you get questions that "stop you in your tracks" (that is, questions where you're not able to help the customer)?

- On a scale from 1 to 10, how many times do customers tell you, "Hey, thanks, you did a great job"?

- What frustrates you most about your customers?

- If you could, how would you fix that frustration?

- What suggestions might you have for a customer service training program at our company?

- Do you have any special comments, negative or positive, about customer service at our company? (Supply a comment area.)

- Do you feel you have adequate support, clarity, etc., as to how you should respond or react to a specific situation?

- How can you tell when a customer is pleased with the service you delivered?

You get the idea. You'll easily come up with more of your own questions that apply to your own customers. Keeping your questions focused on your own business will help you get more focused answers.

As the analysis is carried out, the priority in reaching the audience becomes obvious. In selecting which groups of attendees deserve emphasis, the more often staff members regularly deal directly with customers, the more training they require and the more they will benefit from customer service training. This is your *target audience.* They should receive a predominant share of the training.

Selecting the employee to train does not need to be difficult. The KISS method we mentioned in this section works wonders. Try the 1-to-10 rating method. If an employee is a high risk with customers, meaning he has greater exposure to your clients, mark that employee a 10. If there's lower exposure, rate him or her a little lower. This allows you to see how many employees have direct exposure to customers and what degree of customer service training they will need.

The real-world approach in selecting audiences for customer service training is to create priorities for target audiences and to set up programs for those who most often interact with customers. Then work your way down to those whose exposure to your customers is less and train them as opportunities permit.

Although circumstances vary greatly from organization to organization, a scheme of preferential audiences can be listed.

Priority One: Customer service, or front line personnel, especially call centers

This audience has primary and ongoing responsibilities for serving customers both on the phone and in person. It is in the front line arena where most customer service defects occur.

Members of Customer Service Departments, managers, sales clerks, checkers, and order takers could be included. These positions offer the most potential for improving whatever deficiencies have been identified in the analysis/needs assessment. It is here that significant corrections can be made in attacking root causes of customer dissatisfaction.

Priority Two: Receptionists

Research shows that 80 percent of all business transactions include a phone call at one time or another. Customers call for information they need about your products and services. They have questions that need to be answered before they do business—before they can become customers.

For this reason, receptionists and similar categories of front line employees should receive ample customer service training.

These classes should begin the first week of employment. Front line employees need ongoing customer service training.

Priority Three: Technical support staff

Depending on the nature of the organization, technical support professionals handle specialized questions from callers before and after the sale.

This group can benefit greatly from understanding the theory and practice of customer service. They should be considered as important as receptionists in the Priority Two classification and should be included in the training schedule as quickly as possible. Functioning more effectively in their customer relationships, they can also contribute considerably to remedying shortcomings in customer satisfaction. In today's electronic world, our "tech" employees may need to concentrate a little more on customer service training. They're used to "talking" to their computers, and now they need to learn how to talk to customers.

 KEY POINT: It is in the front line arena where most customer service defects occur.

Other Considerations

Logistics

Logistics may be a challenge. There are various work shifts to be considered. Some employees work 9:00 to 5:00, others 8:00 to 4:00, while some work midnight to 6:00. In many cases, these employees work in different buildings, cities, and even different states. Scheduling customer service training classes obviously demands time and an almost heroic effort.

Availability of the people attending is also a challenge. Supervisors can often free up only a small portion of their departments to attend classes at any given time. Phones, cash registers, and checkout aisles need to be covered.

As important as customer service training is, other corporate-related training also needs to be considered essential. Realistically, there can be up to a half dozen (some mention more!) *different types* of classes that must be included in today's fully dimensional training program. Each must be provided as time permits, and the training budget for facilitator hours *alone* can often limit what courses can be offered and to which groups.

A Plea to Include Everyone

Everyone in an organization who has the remote chance to have contact with customers should be trained to deal with them and serve them "beyond their needs." All employees need to speak the same customer service language.

Depending on the training capabilities and nature of your organization, the following groups can be considered for training:

- Administrative assistants/secretaries
- Sales department members
- Management/supervisors
- Executives

TELEPHONE DOCTOR® CUSTOMER SERVICE TIP:	Managers must speak the same language as employees.

If staff are expected to exhibit customer service skills and good attitudes, then those who lead need to show them the way it's done.

While most managers and owners *do* understand and provide good customer service, there are those who often feel as though they don't need it—they already know everything. An old saying comes to mind:

When you're through learning . . . you're through!

So once again: Whom should you train? Let me hear it loud and clear: *everyone!*

TELEPHONE DOCTOR® CUSTOMER SERVICE TIP:	It starts at the top!

Customer service *must* start at the top. It must, as we said in our earlier chapters, dribble down; it cannot dribble up. Management needs to carry out the mission of good customer service at your company.

Job Knowledge: Duh!

You'd think this would be a "no-brainer." However, many organizations neglect the job knowledge portion in customer service training. That's unfortunate. Job knowledge, along with attitudes and techniques, is one of the most important components of customer service training. It is difficult, if not impossible, to give good customer service when you don't know about the products or services the company offers.

For instance, in any organization, the "first-contact" customer service personnel (let's personalize her and call her "Mary") must have an awareness or job knowledge of the nature of what her organization provides. Mary also must be sufficiently confident to be able to project this knowledge when customers call or come into her place of business. She does not, however, need to know everything. A small amount of job knowledge goes a long way to avoid poor customer service.

Training ideally works to increase the familiarity and the comfort level in understanding and discussing the product or service of her company. Mary should be able to respond to the most basic questions—the frequently asked questions (FAQs). Every organization has them and knows what they are.

EXAMPLE: My husband and I recently went to Cooperstown, New York, where I delivered a customer service training program to a Customer Service Department of a large company.

At the hotel, I casually asked, "How far are we from the Baseball Hall of Fame?" After I asked that question, I thought to myself, "I wonder how many times that question had been asked." Can you imagine answering the same question over, and over, *and over* again and making it sound as though it's the first time you've heard it? When you ask a question that the employee has heard and answered untold times that day, and it sounds as though you were the first one to ask it, then that's good customer service.

For those questions that become complicated, Mary should know how to shift the situation to someone with more expertise without undue inconvenience to the customer.

Specifically, Mary's job knowledge should consist of the following:

- **The business of the company**—such as how it functions; how she fits into the personnel scheme; and how she should be able to use this information when needed

- **The specific job situation**—such as what range of knowledge she is expected to acquire in her individual niche in her department or section; what resources she has for finding more information; and what her responsibility is in obtaining these sources

- **Product/service utilization**—such as how her customers use what they buy from the organization; how her customers can maximize the value from the items or services purchased; and common problems that her customers could experience in using them (This area is key to enhancing the sales/profit ratio because it converts prospects into long-term, repeat customers!)

- **Employee reference list** (by department if possible)— should give names and extensions of employees who can help with facts, questions, and general information employees may need when providing customer service

In addition, Mary should have clear ideas of related matters such as the standards of achievement expected of her; the evaluation criteria that will influence her performance review; and a sense of what constitutes professionalism in the organization.

And clearly, Mary should know the name of the president of her company!

Here's an amazing true story:

A while back, we had a minor inconvenience with a major corporation. We were, in my mind, a good customer. It didn't matter that we weren't a big customer; my perception was that we were a good customer. After all, we used their products didn't we? I decided I would write a letter to the president of this corporation. I made a phone call to the local corporate office and explained to the person who answered, "I'm going to write a letter to the president of your company. Can you please tell me his name?"

"Sure can't," came a very rapid response.

"Excuse me," I said in disbelief. "I only want to know who is the president of your company."

"Don't know for sure," came the response in the same rapid motion. With, I might add, NO OFFER OF WHERE TO GO FOR THE INFORMATION.

Not one to give up easily, I decided to call another local office. Same story. To make a long story short, it took me four phone calls to get the name of the president of this corporation. NO ONE KNEW WHO THE PRESIDENT OF THAT COMPANY WAS (if this was e-mail, then, yes, the capital letters denote I'd be screaming).

In total disbelief, I called the Wall Street Journal and told them that story. They thought enough of it to put it in one of their columns. Can you imagine not knowing the name of the president of the company you work for? That's not even job knowledge—that's common sense.

An effective customer service training program provides knowledge about these and a volume of similar subjects all of which accumulatively produce the desired excellence in Mary and others in her firm who function in the front line.

The Telephone Doctor® principle is that, except for proprietary financial information, there is little about an organization that a highly motivated employee shouldn't learn and know about!

TELEPHONE DOCTOR® CUSTOMER SERVICE TIP:	Train your personnel to know the name of the president or owner of your company. Top management names should be easy to refer to.

Barriers to Training: Uncovering the Obstacles

What would logically stop a customer service training program from being successful? Think for a moment about the barriers, or the problems, that can diminish the quality of customer service training:

- Lack of training resources
- Not having clearly defined procedures
- Unfamiliarity with training content
- Unavailability of attendees
- An inadequate training site

Ask any veteran facilitator about the obstacles they've faced through the years and the list seems to go on and on.

However, the two barriers to training that are most frequently cited as primary causes of troubles are

- the lack of support by management and
- the lack of interest in the program by attendees.

You may be able to overcome content and delivery, but you will need to deal with the issues above. The predicaments of facilities, resources, and the rest can normally be overcome one way or another. However, this is not always so with the lack of management endorsement and attendee enthusiasm.

Getting through to these two groups can boost the value of customer service training by removing what are commonly considered the two most frustrating barriers to training. If you want customer service training and find it difficult to "sell it to management," you need to find out exactly what the concerns are. Otherwise, it is very possible the customer service training won't work.

Please refer to the article located at the end of the Evaluation section later in this book: "Why Your Training Didn't Work," by David Friedman.

Management Involvement: A Must!

Fact: To succeed in your customer service training, you need management involvement and support.

Involvement of managers, decision makers, and top management is particularly important if the customer service training program is expected to change the customer service culture. It is this level of the organization that will decide or approve customer service values, policies, and procedures. Remember that even if it is not written down, there is generally a clearly "acted-upon" level of values that can be articulated. Policies and procedures also may not be written down, but there may be informal policies and procedures in place that have not been captured yet in print. The dialogue you generate with top management around these points could result in an improved context within which you can conduct the training.

When you read the chapter on barriers to training, you'll notice that management often becomes that barrier.

I interviewed a potential Telephone Doctor® client for this section. She had previewed our training programs and felt they were the best for the job that needed to be done. Her letter to our account executive was very sad. She was told by senior management, ". . . train the employees to think and feel the same way *you* do . . . but don't spend any money doing it."

She asked, "If management feels that I am competent and wants people to work with the same ethics and standards as I do, then why won't they trust me to do the training they need?" Why not let her invest in the training package she feels is most valuable? "It is," she says, "the only way I can guarantee their success."

Her closing comment that "we are failing miserably . . . and losing market share" makes a very strong case to let facilitators determine and acquire what they feel is the best program for the employees and the employer. They have the hands-on experience to know what their employees need.

Having management tell you "no," or not being able to budget what you need, is like making a cake without all the proper ingredients. You won't get the results you want.

The facilitator, who is with a reputable and large company, is going to need to "market," *to sell,* a customer service training program to management. Someone within the management team may feel it's not important enough, doesn't want to spend the money, or perhaps doesn't feel as though the service needs to be improved.

At first glance, facilitators find it frustrating that it's often necessary to push a customer service training program to gain its acceptance. Its value is so apparent! Why should there be a need to *sell* it to those who can benefit from it?

If management wants only "smile" training, then the response to that is quite different from whether they truly want a change in the corporate culture. Desiring a change in the organizational culture will require you to look at all systems that support the corporate functions, management practices, and procedures as you select content for the training.

Promoting to Management

You *should* promote the course to managers and supervisors. Then hype the course to those who are scheduled to attend (see "Selling the Training to the Attendees" for some thoughts on how to promote training to attendees).

How should you get managers' and supervisors' attention? If you're not able to get an appointment to sit down and discuss the customer service priorities with a top manager, send a simple memo or letter. For managers, written promotions are normally the most expedient format. In many organizations, it is the *only* way to reach executives, middle managers, and even some supervisors. They're frequently not accessible with calls or a focus group meeting.

If the number of managers is limited, a personally addressed form letter might work, or a standard memo or flyer could be used.

This approach indicates the value of the course to the organization and to the departments and the staff members who will attend. Try opening the communication with a brief statement about the title and the content of the course. Then explain its objective. The closing should be a plea for support of the program by managers and supervisors.

EXAMPLE: While your staff will realize how much they will benefit from these lessons on improved customer service, they may tend to approach the training with greater anticipation if you were to emphasize to them the importance of the experience. Take a moment, if you would, to stress the value of the course to them and to the XYZ organization.

There are fancier approaches involving a newsletter format with articles on the importance of customer service, on training employees to serve the organization's customers, and on the specific benefit to the company and all who participate in the course. As space permits, information about the content of the lessons of the training course could be added.

Perhaps an easy way to promote customer service training would be to use e-mail. Top executives of most organizations can be reached in this way. Even in smaller companies, there are intranet possibilities. A brief announcement of the course and one or two sentences requesting a push from management to their staff who will attend could do the trick.

TELEPHONE DOCTOR® CUSTOMER SERVICE TIP:	Management's backing is key for the support of your customer service training program. For customer service training to succeed, management needs to be involved.

Design
Component

Design:
Not as Scary as it Sounds

Design is the second phase of the overall process of putting together a customer service training program. In this phase, you use all the information gathered in the analysis phase and decide what (content) you will include and how (delivery) you will present it in preparation for the class.

In designing your customer service training, consider the following:

- Your overall outcome
- The content (what you will be teaching), including the following:
  — All games
  — Activities
  — Role playing
- Resources
- The training outline

In defining your overall outcome, decide what you want to be different between what you're doing now and what needs to be done.

The answer (or answers) to this question will determine the content, how you deliver the program, the resources needed, as well as how many training sessions will be necessary to accomplish the training outline.

The content is the "meat and potatoes" of the training sessions. It is the "stuff" to be taught and learned. The content includes the information and skills that you want your employees to leave the training classes knowing and being able to do. Notice the distinction between "knowing" and "doing." It is important to know these distinctions as you design your training, because it will influence the way that you present the content.

The customer service training design is the road map of how you'll pull together the content, how you will deliver it, and what resources you need to achieve the desired outcome.

Here are some big picture training outlines to consider:

1. "Tell 'em" Model:
   - Tell 'em what ya gonna tell 'em.
   - Tell 'em.
   - Tell 'em what ya told 'em.

This model is *exactly* as it appears. It is a great reminder to the facilitator to set the stage for the training, do the training, and remind the students of what you have covered.

2. The "W-H" Model:
   - Who?
   - What?
   - How?
   - When?
   - Where?

This is the most generic of process models but is a great way to start designing the training outline. This model reminds you of *who* is to be trained, *what* they need to learn, *how* they need to learn it, *when* they train, and *where* the training will take place.

While there may be more involved models for training outlines, most are built on the same assumptions as these. But why make it more difficult than you need to? These models can also be used for problem solving customer service concerns and issues.

"W-H" Model Sample:

Who: Customer service reps (12)

What: Say "please" and "thank you"

How: Audio/visuals and role play

When: First Tuesday of each month

Where: Training room No. 3

 KEY POINT: *What* will be different as a result of this program?

Content:
The Stuff They Learn

Content is *what* you will teach in the training classes.

The content is determined after the analysis—after you have determined what the gap is between where you are and where you want to be in relation to customer service. After you have analyzed the information, you are ready to identify what is needed to respond to the gaps.

When you consider what the content will be, you have three choices. You can

- **adapt** a program;
- **acquire** (purchase) a program; or
- **create** a program.

Adapting

Customer service is such an "evergreen" subject, with a never-ending need for training, that adapting is a realistic possibility. You may have access to past customer service training that was previously presented in your organization. These materials should be reviewed carefully to determine if they have the potential for modification and use in the customer service program being planned. Often, a portion of the content can be salvaged.

The task in this case would be to rework the applicable content to fit the current customer service training objective. Before deciding to adapt the content, first consider whether the existing program can be used with only minimal revisions. Then identify the revisions required and write them out in outline form. Finally, consider whether the training objective will be met with the product as reworked. It makes sense to consider using pre-existing content only when minor modifications are needed.

What process is most effective in the makeover of existing materials? You can begin by making the most obvious changes. Revise titles and case study settings so that they conform to the lesson objective. Then proceed to major changes as necessary. It is helpful to record each of these on a list of "change notes." This statement then becomes the guiding document to the revisions.

Acquiring

Off-the-shelf packages seem to be the easiest and most common approach and are available from a variety of sources.

The components of these packages differ, but typically they contain the **lesson content** in a specific format, such as a text manual, audio, DVD, etc. In addition, they can offer a **facilitator's guide** that indicates how the customer service training package can be used most effectively and often includes attendee **workbooks.** Various training aids are often included or are available from the package producer. These include study aids, on-the-job reference cards, self-evaluation, and the like.

Off-the-shelf packages you acquire are valuable because they save initial preparation time. The best packages are repeatedly tested in classroom situations and revised regularly to improve the content and the graphics. The product is usually highly professional and the choices are numerous.

There are very few downsides to using these ready-made packages, which is why they are the most frequently used method of putting together a customer service training program.

In many cases, the customer service training package is DVD based. If this is the case at your organization, you could create introductory commentary that links the content of the DVD with your specific lesson plan.

Most customer service training programs you will acquire are called generic. They are made to fit a variety of organizations, and, in truth, they are a lot of fun and can be very challenging. You can easily use a customer service training program that is generic and make it *just* for your organization. That's where the role playing and skill practice comes into play.

As someone who needs to put a customer service training class together quickly, your time may be better spent on other areas rather than trying to create something that has already been done for you. In other words, why "reinvent the wheel"? Acquiring the material and using training experts are good choices. Even when you are creating a custom program, you can acquire some information and expertise to add to it.

Creating

Of the three methods of developing content for lessons (adapting existing materials, acquiring new or off-the-shelf materials, and creating materials), the decision to create relatively new content involves a highly detailed investigation of the subject.

Facilitators who are not familiar with customer service report that they may need to devote a significant amount of time and effort to acquire a feel for the material to be included. This is why creating a customer service training program is so challenging.

Experienced customer service managers have a firm grasp on the subject but may need to think through what should be in the lessons.

There is also the need to consider the teaching materials that will supplement the lessons: workbooks, handouts, DVDs, audios, overheads, and slides.

In creating your own customer service training, you'll need to consider some practical information:

1. What are your organization's values, policies, procedures, and management preferences regarding customer service? This information can be helpful in making your customer service design plan applicable to any industry or type of organization. If values are not clearly available, look at your organization's mission statement.

2. What are the interpersonal and intrapersonal skills needed to support an exemplary customer service environment? The topics covered generally relate to such skills as listening, dealing with difficult customers, and communicating clearly.

3. What are the best customer service practices? You can do your own research by identifying leading organizations similar to yours and contacting them; what are some of their most successful customer service practices?

4. Create "what if" scenarios that allow students to practice skills learned.

Creating your own customer service training program can be very rewarding, but it is a challenge in terms of time and materials. At first sight, this may seem to be the most economical method but can frequently prove to be the opposite.

Budget:
What's It Gonna Cost Me?

Customer service training budgets are made similarly to your personal budget. In other words, make a list of the things you think you'll need and then add a place for the "unexpected." This is an obvious must-have category even in a household budget (well, at least in mine).

Not having a budget plan in mind for customer service training will cost you more in the long run. Larger companies, of course, are guided by their budgets. They make them annually; they're prepared well in advance. They know exactly what they intend to spend. They have big departments and lots of people making these budgets, not only for customer service training, but also for the entire company.

Budgets for customer service training can range from $50 to $100,000 (sometimes more). It depends on what you're going to do in the training and how much the company is willing to devote to this area.

There are companies that look at customer service training as something they can do without. There are companies that consider customer service training as optional, and they eliminate their Training Department altogether. Those are the companies that probably need it the most.

If you think of customer service training as an expense, something you *cannot* afford to do, you could be starting off on the wrong foot. Training is an investment.

Companies frequently seem to mouth the same slogans. Have you seen these signs when you shop?

> "The customer comes *first!*"
> "We *love* the customer!"
> "The customer is *number one!*"
> *Blah, blah, blah . . .*

Many companies put a lot of money into banners and signs that say all of the above, yet may not focus on customer service training. The banners and signs are far more effective when the company supports them with training. I've been in plenty of companies that have those banners and I have received poor service.

TELEPHONE DOCTOR® CUSTOMER SERVICE TIP:	Support your banners with customer service training!

When people tell me they would love to do customer service training, but it's too expensive, I wonder if it's just an excuse. Do they really mean they don't have the time, or maybe (frequently the case) aren't aware of how to start their customer service training?

As we mentioned, customer service training can start with zero dollars and can go up into the hundreds of thousands of dollars.

What do *you* want to spend on customer service training? Some companies don't have a single idea of what they should spend on training, or even where customer service training costs start.

That's right. The cost of *not* training in the customer service arena can be costlier in dollars than the training itself.

Let's talk about the actual prices.

Don't have a training budget? How does *free* sound? Just talking with your staff about what to do and what not to do is a start—a slow start, but a *start.* Decide on planned customer service training; it will really pay off. Spending a few minutes each morning with the employees who are going to be interacting with the customers is a start.

Your public library or community college both have "no cost" training available. There may be dozens of customer service training materials: books, audios, DVDs, and the like at your local library. One of the key benefits of using this facility is if you see what you like, you can contact the company that wrote it or produced it, and see what else it offers.

Okay, no more "I can't afford it." You *can* afford *free.* You *can* afford to do customer service training.

There are, however, some drawbacks to using the public library for customer service training. The free part is great *if* the materials are available. What happens when someone else has checked out what you need? That's not going to be of any value to you or your company. And how soon will you need to return the materials? You certainly won't be able to keep them in your office for any length of time. The library wants them back, and all too quickly.

In most cases, the public libraries do not usually include any workbooks, facilitator's guides, or ancillary materials to hand out for following up. But at least you've made a step to a customer service training program, and we applaud you for that. Your customers will, too.

 KEY POINT: *Not* providing customer service training can be much more expensive than the training itself.

Now let's say you *did* budget customer service training for your company or department. What will your expenses be? Some things you may want to consider in the way of material costs for a classroom training include:

- Do you need paper, pencils, flip charts, TV/DVD player, or overhead projector?
- Will you be showing a DVD or running a computer-based slide presentation?
- Will you be using workbooks?
- Will the training be on site? Off site?
- Will you be serving beverages? Food?

You *may* need an outside location to conduct the training. You *may* need a DVD player, an overhead projector, a laptop computer, or handouts. Take time to make a short, rough list of the items you think you'll need to have on hand in order to conduct customer service training. Here's a simple start:

Item	Estimated Amount You Want to Spend
The room/facility	$ _____
Handouts for approximately 25 people	$ _____
Pencils	$ _____
Paper	$ _____
DVD player	$ _____
DVD	$ _____
Audio player and cassette	$ _____
Overhead projector	$ _____
Computer for CD or DVD	$ _____
Flip chart/white board	$ _____
Markers	$ _____
Workbooks	$ _____
Evaluation sheets	$ _____
Miscellaneous	$ _____
Total:	**$** _____

Think about the other things you'll need or want to have when you put 25 employees (the optimum for a customer service training class) into a room.

Will you be serving any beverages or food? Do you need to purchase paper plates, etc.? Believe it or not, there are some companies that spend more on food for the employees than the customer service training itself.

TELEPHONE DOCTOR® CUSTOMER SERVICE TIP:	Training doesn't cost . . . it pays.

Cost: Electronic Media

Of the three options in developing content for customer service training (adapting, acquiring, and creating), research indicates that off-the-shelf customer service training is the overwhelming choice. It's easy, and it's relatively inexpensive.

DVDs and other electronic media can run anywhere from $49 to $895 and up. Which program you choose depends on your likes and dislikes. There are programs that have a story line with only good points. There are programs that show a wrong way and then a right way.

The best type of customer service program is one that allows the participants to become involved. Remember, we're trying to change behavior. Your input before and after showing a DVD is critical.

Before selecting a program, most companies usually allow you to *preview* what you'll be purchasing. Remember, you will probably be using this program for years. In other words, it's a good idea to look at the price of the program over a length of time. Preview several programs so that you know what you're getting. Compare them and be sure you compare apples to apples.

It's okay to purchase more than one DVD on the same topic. You have two or three pairs of glasses, don't you? And certainly four or five pairs of shoes. No reason you shouldn't have three or four customer service training programs to use within your class. Topics are varied, so you might need one DVD on irate callers and another for basic communication skills. This list can be endless.

A $49 DVD may come with a note of "good luck with your training" from the producer, while a $500 program is frequently accompanied by a facilitator's guide, workbooks, and/or other ancillary materials.

There's an old saying that goes, "You retain half of what you hear, one third of what you read, and most of what you *see.*" That's why training on customer service with visuals comes highly recommended.

Cost: Audio

Using audio programs for customer service training can work for one-on-one training. If, however, your group has five or more members, it's not as effective as other methods, such as a DVD or live presentations. But, within a group setting, audio can be a good assistant to your customer service training in a segmented portion.

Cost-wise, audio programs on customer service are affordable and durable, and they seem to last forever. Only when you lose them do you usually need to buy another. And because of the normally low-cost factor, replacing them doesn't seem to hurt as much. Audios can range from $9.95 for one to $199 for a set of six or eight cassettes.

Cost: The Book

There are literally dozens (maybe hundreds) of books on customer service training in all price ranges. Again, they're good for smaller groups, for one-on-one improvement, and as handy references. *How to Get Your Customers Swearing by You, Not at You: Telephone Doctor's Guide to Customer Service Training* is an example of how easy it can be to implement a program.

Cost: Electronic Media

Numerous electronic media outlets are available, often more economical than face-to-face learning. Why? Companies that host e-learning programs via the Internet can reach hundreds or thousands of individuals at the same time from one remote location, thus saving them costs of time, travel, and facility rental. E-learning is especially good for companies with rural locations, home-based employees, part-time employees, and virtually anyone who has access to a computer.

EDPF: Excuse Me?

EDPF is a mnemonic device that reminds you of crucial steps involved in teaching someone. Anytime teaching takes place, from a child learning to make a bed, to someone learning new customer service skills, the teacher imparts knowledge to that person in a certain way, simply called EDPF:

> Explain
> Demonstrate
> Practice
> Feedback

If the method of teaching is only lecture, then only a certain percentage of learning takes place. If the teaching incorporates "explain" (lecture that can include visual or audio aids) *and* "demonstrate," that would be even better because the demonstration allows the person to see and hear at the same time. If you allow "practice" to happen when the person actually tries to use what was heard and seen, then the learning would go even further. The more senses you add to the customer service training, the more information will be retained and learned.

If you're able, give appropriate feedback, i.e., "You did a great job managing that difficult customer," or "Perhaps you could do it a little better in offering what we can do." The facilitator will know what was taught, learned, or just as importantly, what was *not* learned. Feedback is where the instructor has the opportunity and responsibility to reinforce what was done correctly and to correct what wasn't.

EXAMPLE: Explain the skill:
Tell the attendee to look up a number in a phone book.

Demonstrate the skill:
You show them how you do it.

Practice the skill:
Have the attendees do it.

Feedback:
You did that great! Or
Let's try that again and see if
    we can use another method.

EDPF is one way to teach customer service skills.

TELEPHONE DOCTOR® CUSTOMER SERVICE TIP:	***Ancient Chinese Proverb*** I hear and I forget. I see and I remember. I do and I understand.

Developed for Telephone Doctor® by Joanne Kelly

Getting Started: Let's Go!

Prepare a lesson plan. It becomes the "actions" you will take to address the shortcomings found in your analysis. It combines content and processes and outlines what will happen during the training course. Be it one hour or four hours, you'll need an outline of what's going to happen during the time period. A lesson plan lets you conceptualize the course before beginning the actual presentation. **It is a key factor in presenting customer service training.**

Following is a sample lesson plan. It will show you how easy it can be to create your own customer service training program. For your outline, include four basic headings:

- Instructional material needed
- Equipment and supplies required
- Training methods to be used
- Timetable for the lesson presentation with facilitator notes

NOTE: Wherever you see "Company," personalize it with your own company's or organization's name.

Telephone Doctor®
Sample Lesson Plan
(Outline)

Module:	Training Program, DVD #1
Estimated Time:	90 minutes
Number of Attendees:	Up to 25
Objective/Purpose:	To provide a basic understanding of the program and understand the importance of customer service training for the company

Preparation (Materials Needed):

- DVD and DVD player
- Flip charts
- Markers
- Extra notepaper and pens
- Program evaluation sheets
- Reminder cards

Procedure: The following is a step-by-step guide to a successful customer service training class. Please refer to the Flip Chart Information sheet on pages 61–63 for instructions on setting up your flip charts. Good luck and happy training.

Welcome

Welcome the attendees to the class and introduce yourself. Let them know that the class will be 90 minutes in length.

Icebreaker (See Flip Chart #1)

The purpose of an icebreaker is to get the attendees relaxed and in a learning mode. This icebreaker also serves as a "getting acquainted session" for the attendees. For this exercise, you will start by explaining the flip chart diagram. Each symbol on the flip chart represents something that each attendee will tell about himself or herself. Start with yourself as the example. State the following as you point to the symbols on the flip chart:

- Your name
- Where you were born
- The city you live in now
- Hobbies
- Any pets
- How long you've been with the organization

After everyone has introduced himself or herself, go on to the next step.

The Purpose of This Program (See Flip Chart #2)

Turn the flip chart to the next page and explain the following: The Company has chosen customer service training as a way to prepare us for the future. While the Company is growing rapidly, we need to stay focused on the most important aspect of our business: THE CUSTOMER. In order to survive, the Company must keep itself well beyond the reach of the competition when it comes to the level of customer service we provide. So in order to be consistent with our mission statement, we must continue to be the *best* at everything we do.

The Buy-In (See Flip Chart #3)

On this chart, you will ask the attendees what they think the initials WIIFM stand for. Explain that it is not a radio station; it stands for "What's in it for me?" This is the question anyone has when he or she is introduced to something new. Explain to the class that if they put into practice the things they will learn by attending this training course, the following will occur: (Write the following below the picture of the radio.)

1. **Easier calls:** By making your customers feel comfortable, they will become more relaxed and easier to work with.

2. **Happier customers:** Customers who have enjoyed their contact with you are left with a *positive* attitude toward the Company.

3. **Happy boss:** If the callers are happier and more relaxed, you will be less likely to get a call that you feel you cannot handle, and the boss will not have to calm down any irate or unhappy customers. This will make him/her happy.

4. **A happier workplace:** If you are friendlier on the phone, it will help promote a positive work environment. Remember, we are customers to one another.

Ask attendees why they think each numbered point would occur if the Company provided better customer service. Try to get the attendees to give you these answers. If they need help, use what is written next to the answers and get them to agree or disagree.

Introduce Your First Topic

Give five key points. Point by point, write down on the flip chart any notes that the attendees took regarding each point. If you do not end up getting down all the key points from the class notes, help fill in the blanks with the answers below:

1. **What does a customer want?** (Flip Chart #4) They want a greeting, a welcome, your interest, your knowledge, an assurance, and your thanks. When the Company does each of these things, it gives the customer a feeling of importance that he or she likes to experience. On the second page of Flip Chart #4, have the attendees think of words that start with the corresponding letters in the word CUSTOMER (written vertically). The words that the class members come up with should help identify their definition of excellent customer service.

2. **Is customer service training important?** (The answer is YES.) Everyone should be trained. This key point does not need to be written on a flip chart page. Discuss briefly that we all know that training is essential in providing excellent customer service.

3. **Automatic door mentality.** (Flip Chart #5) Help make it easy to do business with the Company. For this point, we will first identify some of the things that the Company does in order to promote an automatic door mentality. (Have the attendees give you ideas to write down on the chart. For example: "One call does it all" or "same day shipping," etc.) After you identify the things the Company does, ask the attendees what they can do as associates to help promote this mentality. These answers might include friendly customer service, following up with problems, taking care of every customer to the best of your abilities, etc.

4. **Customer appreciation.** (Flip Chart #6) Customer appreciation is not merely a part of excellent customer service, but the very essence of it. If everything you do tells your customer they're appreciated, the service they receive will be consistently excellent. Have the attendees fill in the blank spaces of the Consistency Chart.

5. **It's fun to be good!** (This can be written at the bottom of Flip Chart #6.) Reinforce to the attendees that it is not always easy to be good, but when you're good, it's fun.

Evaluation

Pass out evaluation sheets for the attendees to complete and collect them before they leave.

Summary

This program is not an event, it's a *process*. Old habits are hard to break, but with practice and reinforcement, your bad habits can be changed into business-friendly habits. These ideas are fun and easy and will help make your job at the Company more enjoyable. It starts with *you*. Remember that consistency is important. No one is perfect, but if you are consistent, you're on the right path. Be *consistently* friendly to your customers. Pass out reminder cards. Tell the attendees that these cards should be kept at their desks (in plain view) so that they can be used to remind them of all the things a customer should receive when they call the company.

Flip Chart Information
for the Lesson Plan

Cover Sheet for Flip Chart

Welcome to the [your company] Customer Service Training
Program

Flip Chart #1

Draw a picture of a name tag, a stork, a house, a
baseball and bat, a cat or dog, and a calendar.

Flip Chart #2

Write out: Company Mission Statement:
*"To be the best (industry/supplier) in the world
as measured by associates, customers, owners,
and suppliers . . . through excellent customer
service."*

Flip Chart #3

For this chart, try your best to draw a picture
of a radio. In the middle of the drawing write the
initials WIIFM (What's in it for ME?) This is the
"buy-in" portion of this presentation. You are
trying to get the attendees to believe in what they
are about to see and convince them that it *will*
help make their job more enjoyable. Follow the
instructions under the "buy-in" section of the
training plan for the rest of this chart.

Flip Chart #4 (2 pages)

On the first page of Flip Chart #4, write "What does a customer want?" Give the class a chance to answer what they think a customer wants and what the video proposed. Write down the answers and the feedback you get from the class. On the second page of the flip chart, write the word CUSTOMER vertically along the left side of the page. Starting with the letter C, have the associates give you words that start with the letter C and that describe what a customer wants. Do the same thing for the rest of the letters. After you get the words for each letter, review what the group came up with and how it relates to the first flip chart. The words that the class comes up with should help you reinforce what a customer wants from a business.

Flip Chart #5

At the top of the chart, write "Automatic Door Mentality." Draw a line down the middle of the page. At the top of the first column, write our company's name. At the top of the second column, write "YOU." Start with the Company column and have the class give you examples of things that our company does as a business that make it easy for customers to do business with us—things like same-day shipping, one call does it all, etc. After you have established what our company does, ask the class what *we* can do, as associates, to help promote and maintain an automatic door mentality (customer contact should be friendly and professional, thank our customers, give them our full attention, etc.).

Flip Chart #6

You may use the Telephone Doctor® Consistency Chart. The answers are as follows:

> When you lose consistency, you lose quality.
>
> When you lose quality, you lose customers.
>
> When you lose customers, you lose jobs.
>
> When you lose jobs, you're history.

Have the attendees help you fill in the blanks. Reinforce how important consistency is when servicing the customer.

Consistency Counts

When you lose . . .	You lose . . .
CONSISTENCY	
	YOU'RE HISTORY!! Goodbye!

Nancy Friedman, Telephone Doctor®, 1993

Resources: Where Do I Find the Good Stuff to Help Me?

Ancillary Materials

In training, the term *ancillary materials* usually means the "stuff that comes with the program." So when you purchase training materials (or adapt or create them), verify that you have the ancillary materials needed. Webster says it more eloquently by defining *ancillary* as "that which supplements."

Ancillary materials may consist of a facilitator's guide, attendee workbooks, overheads, audio recordings, DVDs, flip charts, handouts, desktop reminder cards, and any other item that successfully enhances the training.

Their purpose is to

- enliven instruction;
- break up lectures; and
- reinforce important points of the training.

However, we would like to offer a word of warning on copyrights on ancillary materials:

If you like the program you purchased and want another copy, purchase it. Do not make a copy of the program. It's difficult to think you have purchased an audio recording, a DVD, software, or a book and then find out you're not able to duplicate it. It's yours, isn't it? You paid for it, didn't you? Well, you paid for the material, in a manner of speaking, but the information on the media belongs to the person who wrote it.

We've dedicated a chapter just to copyright (see page 81). It will enlighten those who may not realize what a copyright notice means.

Some other resources that can be used within your customer service training include the following:

Audio/Visual

Audio recordings and DVDs are available from most producers of instructional materials and can be purchased for a reasonable cost to enliven a training program. Audio recordings and DVDs are fun and a good add-on to most customer service training.

Books

There are all sorts of customer service training books on the market. When you have time, check out the Potpourri chapter (see page 147) and see all the related customer service associations. Each one of them offers dozens of applicable books on customer service.

Books can be used as ancillary material. Finding a good customer service quote by someone you value in the industry can give what you say an enormous amount of credibility.

Handouts

Handouts are easy to acquire. Newspaper and magazine articles, headlines, illustrations from books, and information from the Internet are excellent sources of handouts. With imagination, any number of items can be used to strengthen the content of the lessons. (Be sure to provide attribution when using materials from such sources.)

One reminder: When developing and gathering instructional materials, be certain to indicate on the master lesson plan *when* these are to be quoted, cited, and/or handed out. In this way, they can be *ideally timed to highlight* what is being taught.

Overheads/PowerPoint® Slides

Today, in the high-tech age, we have the computer—complex graphics, clip art programs, color printers, and copiers. Overheads, however, still represent the functional option for creating what you want in instructional aids.

Overheads can also be adapted, if necessary, with minimal effort and time from other programs. New overhead masters can be created with relative ease.

Either way, overheads represent a prime opportunity to reinforce an important point in the lecture and/or discussion without a major expense or time investment. Experienced facilitators can select critical concepts in the lesson for overhead emphasis.

There is a tendency to use small fonts and graphics when preparing overheads. Please remember that an overhead is not a magnifying glass, so use larger letters than normal so that the text is readable from the rear of the room. Also try to avoid putting the sequel to *Gone with the Wind* on each overhead. Short, bulleted comments make the most sense.

TELEPHONE DOCTOR® CUSTOMER SERVICE TIP:	Do not simply read from your overheads or PowerPoint slides. To do so could render you useless.

PowerPoint is a registered trademark of Microsoft®.

Icebreakers: Fun and Games

Icebreakers are the fun part of customer service training.

They are short, fun games at the beginning of a training session that can help reduce tension or frustration and help get everyone in a good mood. An icebreaker can be as simple as taking turns and telling everyone your name, where you were born, and one interesting fact about yourself, to a more intricate version of getting people out of their chairs and moving around the room. They help both the facilitator and the attendees warm up the group. Rather than just starting on the training, you start out having fun. It makes sense.

How lessons are introduced can make a difference in the attitude of attendees and the success of the entire customer service training process. This quick activity is designed to help attendees get acquainted with you and each other. It requires only a short time, sets a positive tone, and creates an informal and relaxed feeling.

Icebreakers work whether the group members know one another or are complete strangers. It's sometimes good to have the facilitator take part in the icebreaker. A few minutes taken at the beginning of any program will help create good feelings. Listening carefully to what each person offers as personal background (and the manner in which he or she expresses this) also provides clues for later use in reaching each member of the class in subsequent training sessions.

One proven successful icebreaker approach is to divide class members into pairs and have them interview each other. Have the "interviewers" take turns asking their newly assigned partner questions about their work, family, hobbies, and reasons for attending. You also could prepare in advance simple questions for them to ask each other, because sometimes attendees get stage fright and aren't able to think of their own questions when put on the spot.

An icebreaker perfect for customer service training is to ask the audience to tell you about their worst customer service experience. In my interviews with clients for this book, 80 percent said that's how they start their customer service training class. It doesn't have to be a "nightmare" either; it could be about their *best* customer service experience or their most unusual customer request. Again, you'll be able to pick up nuances about how attendees view their work from some of the answers they give.

Icebreakers, in one form or another, can be used before *each* lesson in the course. Your imagination is your only limitation. There are numerous books on this subject. Many of the ideas are really quite clever and worth the time to learn and use. Icebreakers are fun!

Housekeeping:
Where's the Bathroom?

"Excuse me, where's the bathroom?"

You're going to hear this—a lot. Like so many things, it's best to handle the question before it's asked.

Because some housekeeping items are routine, they often can be overlooked. But as we well know, breakdowns or defects in the details of class sites and presentations create distractions. For reasons we can only guess, attendees seem to welcome disturbances of any kind. Give attendees half a chance and away they go to check messages and voice mails, get a refreshment, carry on conversations, and so on. Then you need to take time from what should be productive customer service training to try to get them back on track—what a waste of time and effort.

To help ensure that training goes smoothly, develop and use a housekeeping checklist:

- The training area is neat, uncluttered, and distraction free.
- The heating and air-conditioning comfort level is controlled to the best degree possible.
- The lighting is adequate, without glare.
- Noise and interruptions can be controlled.
- Break times are planned with mention made of the convenience of restrooms and smoking areas.
- The seating arrangement (classroom, conference table, theater, etc.) is conducive to the lesson of that day.
- Coffee and snacks are available.

- Instructional equipment is functioning. (Test all audio/ visual equipment, computer, overhead projector, and tape recorder *beforehand.* Remember to check the electrical outlets, too.)

- Make sure the flip chart and markers are handy.

- Be sure DVDs, slides, and other audio/visual aids are easily accessible and—this is important—are in the order you need at the right time in the training class! It's very frustrating to have a series of visuals in the wrong order.

Depending on the circumstances of the training, the checklist can be amended to fit the specific needs of the lesson. After the first class, most facilitators, we bet, have such an inventory in mind, if not on paper. After a time, use of this type of reminder becomes automatic. Still, don't overlook the checklist. It can contribute to a facilitator's confidence in lesson delivery. Without a checklist, no matter how many times you present a program, it's possible to overlook an item.

Facilitator's Guides

Facilitator's guides lead the facilitator through the training activity. They essentially comprise the details about what the facilitator will do during the instructional process. In format, they usually consist of an outline of the content with notes and procedures alongside. The result is a "play book."

While there's no standardized format for the facilitator's guide, it should be developed in a way to ensure a link between the lesson's objective and the facilitator's activities. Some consist of exceedingly detailed directions, while others are merely sketches.

Working from the highlights of the content on one side of the page, the adjacent commentary and notations present reminders of activities, exercises, and tips for the instructor when presenting lessons. The appropriate method of presentation, such as lecture, discussion, or role play, is usually noted with each segment of the lesson.

Other notes specify training resources, supplies, equipment, facilities, and other support materials needed for the training exercise. Some support materials include DVDs, audio, computer-generated slide presentations, overheads, handouts, bibliographies, reference aids, and the like. The equipment needed to employ these materials could be noted as well as personal notes to the facilitator.

The resulting document becomes a very detailed guide for what to do, how to do it, and specifically what mechanically is required to accomplish the training.

The format can be whatever is workable for the facilitators. Some prefer a very detailed statement, others need only a few reference points as clues. In customer service, any variation in format would be applicable, as long as it serves the needs of the specific facilitator.

Workbooks for Attendees: Make it Easy for Attendees to Learn

The material in participants' workbooks varies as widely as the facilitator's guides. Typically they contain the overall lesson objective, subobjectives for the lesson's segments, highlights of the program's content, print versions of handouts, activity lists, quizzes, and space for notes.

A standard participants' workbook will include the following:

- A statement of the program's purpose—"what's in it for you (attendee)?"
- How to get the most from the lesson and from the workbook
- A before-and-after skills inventory
- Activity areas with review questions
- Quizzes
- Key points in summary

Here are some things to look for in the participants' workbooks:

Workbooks should be easy to read and follow and not jam packed with extraneous material that would hinder their use. Attendees (and the rest of us) are reluctant to read a lot, especially when the data is presented in a solid, overwhelming text fashion. The pages should invite readership. They should be lean and mean and attractive in appearance, with white space and suitable illustrations and diagrams. Make sure that using the workbook is not a chore. **Be sure to number the pages**.

Remember, when using workbooks during your customer service training lessons, be specific about what you're referring to so that the attendees are able to find their places, ask questions, and take notes. Allow them enough time to keep pace in their workbooks. Suggest how the workbook can be helpful to them as a reminder of the lesson's points when they're back on the job or as a source of information for independent study.

Role Playing:
So You Want to Be in Movies!

Through the years, we've found that role playing—though many attendees do not enjoy the thought of doing it—is one of the more successful techniques in customer service training. After all, in customer service role playing, attendees can act out real-world situations they are likely to encounter.

The process involves the facilitator presenting the role play scenario and asking for volunteers to play the roles (not always an easy task). The facilitator provides the ground rules, behaviors, reactions, and the like. Then the role players act out the scenario, and the entire class analyzes the role play.

Here are two approaches for role playing.

The first approach allows players to think, speak, and behave like someone else. Being an irate customer is a natural for customer service training. This teaches the attendees to identify with other people and their problems and to appreciate different perspectives.

In the second approach, the players are themselves and can report a particularly frustrating experience that they have had as customers.

While role playing can be conducted in pairs or small groups, the procedure is quite effective when staged in front of the entire class. Therefore, all attendees can find ways to handle the roles. Alternative solutions can be tried, which reflect company policies and basic methods of diffusing hostility.

A way to enhance role playing is to use probing questions on "What happened here?" during the analysis of the role play to guide attendees to arrive at workable solutions:

- How well can you predict the reactions of the customers?
- How else might the situation be managed?
- What effective approaches have you used?
- What, in summary, can we learn from this?

Be careful that the role playing doesn't go on and on in one scenario. Make sure you give the "players" a time line. Three minutes is more than enough time for one scene— it loses effect when carried on too long. While we realize we're not working with Oscar-winning performances, the employees who are selected to do the role playing need to be sufficiently extroverted and confident to carry off the session. Some attendees may feel uncomfortable with leading the role playing. And some role playing exercises will involve previous knowledge of the situation on the part of the employee.

Of all the class participation exercises, role playing is typically the *least* liked activity by the attendees. Volunteers can be scarce. Sometimes when you choose your players, resentment or reluctance may be evident. One fair way to involve *everyone* would be to put the attendees' names in a bowl and have half of the audience each pick a name to find who they will partner up with in the role playing. You can also have a ready-made list of "scenarios" they can choose from. A few examples of role playing would be:

1. The store employee has just told you the item you want is out of stock. That's all he/she has said.

2. When calling a company, you're trying to reach a human being and all you get is the automated attendant. Finally, someone answers. You want to know why you are not able to reach a human.

3. You're trying to purchase an item, and the person assisting you only gives you one-word answers.

4. You're waiting for someone to help you. After waiting in line for several minutes, you see the clerk fiddling with paperwork and ignoring you. When you ask if you could please be helped, you are told to, "hang on a sec, I'll be right with you."

If these role-playing scenarios seem close to home, it's because all of them have happened to your employees, to *me,* and to *you.* Bring the real world to the customer service training class. Start saving bad customer service incidents that happen to you. It could be someone rude on the phone or an in-person visit at a location that has frustrated you.

Remember, have fun with role playing. Let the participants use funny props. It's okay if they go overboard (your customers sometimes do).

Role playing demands some skill and practice on the part of the facilitator. Deft handling of your participants is definitely needed. You'll feel an enormous sense of accomplishment when you get an attendee who did not want to role play up in front and pretending he or she is someone else.

Remember, it's just role playing! Don't take it too seriously.

Copyright: Do NOT Use Intellectual Property without Asking Permission!

Are you going to be using purchased training material?

Does a copyright notice appear anywhere on the introductory pages? On a footnote? In an appendix? Anywhere? Make the effort to thoroughly check for a notice to ensure that the re-use of any existing material does not violate stated copyright provisions. Even if the content was purchased years ago and used at that time, a note to the copyright holder will safely determine any restrictions concerning its revision.

When writing the copyright holder to obtain permission for using the material, indicate how it will be used. On occasions, there may be a charge for this, but usually it won't be as much as the cost of the original product. Obviously, it makes sense that this request should be sent off and permission received in writing before you devote a lot of time and trouble into the reworking. In many cases, you may learn that special permission may not be needed, but the extra step is always a good safeguard.

Imagine this scary scenario:

> You've just received notice from your company's attorney that a major video training company is seeking $190,000 in penalties and fines. The reason? The new facilitator you just hired in the Seattle office, eager to complete a new customer service training assignment quickly, is duplicating DVDs.
>
> Someone found this out and reported it to the producer.
>
> Now you must find an extra $190,000 in the budget or face the humiliation of litigation.

This could happen to you! In fact, it's happening all over corporate America and the world.

Most organizations don't deliberately try to steal copyrighted training programs. In fact, many aren't aware they're doing something wrong. In a techno-happy generation, copying all types of electronic media seems to be as harmless as lending a friend your DVD of a popular TV program from the night before. The penalties for copyright violators are tough and are getting tougher.

The problem comes from a lack of education, particularly over understanding the term *ownership* in relation to copyrighted, educational material. When you buy a DVD program, you only own the rights to *show* that DVD. The educational material on that DVD is, and remains, the property of the copyright owner. You do not own the DVD in the traditional sense of "owning."

Following are some basic steps that corporations can take to protect themselves and their companies from a potential copyright lawsuit:

1. When you use a DVD program, it would be wise to open every training session with a reminder to the class that it is illegal to duplicate a DVD. Personalize that reminder with *your* company name: "It is against the policies of ABC Company to duplicate copyright material." This will help educate your employees. Remember, what they don't know *can* hurt you.

2. Don't fast forward over the copyright warning at the beginning or end of any electronic media. Repetition is the mother of learning.

3. Let your branch offices know that it is *always illegal* to duplicate training programs. Away from the watchful eyes at corporate headquarters, duplicating DVDs seems somehow "less illegal." It's *always* against the law to copy a DVD without the expressed, written permission of the producer.

82

4. Keep track of your corporate training library. If it suddenly seems to be reproducing, you've got a problem.

5. "But no one will ever know." Wrong! A major source of lawsuit action is the disgruntled former employee with an axe to grind. Most producers offer substantial rewards for information leading to copyright offenses.

6. Write or call the producer/publisher of the material for information on understanding your specific legal rights once you have purchased a training program.

Some facilitators are concerned about losing expensive training programs from overuse or through damage. DVDs are extremely durable. In the unlikely event of damage, most DVD producers will make a replacement available within 24 hours. This alleviates the need to ever make a "back-up" or archival copy.

It's not all bad news. Most companies are "squeaky clean." They start from an ethical foundation. For others, it's simply a matter of honor.

Considering the huge value that our society places on intellectual property, there is a large deficit in the public's understanding of the laws and the control placed on copy-righted works. It doesn't matter if you have purchased a copy of the latest popular DVD, a Microsoft® software program, or a customer service training program, these products are all copyrighted and licensed to you, the end user, under specific terms and conditions.

If we expect to be entertained by the finest movies, benefit from productive operating systems, or train with the best customer service techniques, then it's of vital importance that we understand and respect the issues surrounding the use of these copyrighted works.

TELEPHONE DOCTOR® CUSTOMER SERVICE TIP:	Remember to give credit where credit is due.

 KEY POINT: Illegal use of protected intellectual property can carry substantial fines.

Delivery
Component

Delivery: The Fun Part

You've *analyzed* your needs, *designed* the customer service training, and now it's time to *deliver* it.

Delivery is *presenting* the customer service training content that you designed. As you plan the delivery of the customer service training, remember it is a process with many considerations and not just a one-time event. In organizations where the goal has been to change the culture, it truly becomes a way of life.

Many first-time facilitators ask for presentation skills. That's good because *how* you present can be as important as *what* you present. Let's go over the *how,* and then we'll cover the *what.*

EXAMPLE: Pick a song. Any song. Let's say you chose Tony Bennett's signature song, "I Left My Heart in San Francisco." If I had the sheet music and sang the song and THEN we played Tony Bennett's version, you'd hear quite a difference. Aside from the talent aspect (I'm not able to carry a tune), one notable difference would be in the delivery—how each word was handled, emphasized, and delivered. Yet why? We both had the same lyrics, didn't we?

If you're going to be delivering the customer service training information, you'll want to get as good as you can with your delivery.

Your emphasis, believability, enthusiasm, and conviction all enter into your delivery and the success of the program.

There are several things to consider in determining how you will present and deliver the content:

- The customer service training program design
- The audience
- The training environment

The **customer service training program design** is your road map for how you will deliver. Some facilitators use detailed notes, and others use very sketchy outlines. *All* outlines are what the facilitator needs to accomplish and how they will do it. Notes can be placed on the facilitator's outline to prompt certain stories or remind them to use certain audio/visual aids. The use of colored markers and stickers can also help in prompting the facilitator. Also be prepared to make adjustments in your design as you learn who will be in each session.

The **audience** is the *who*. Who will be in the training session? When considering the *who,* pay attention to overall educational levels of the anticipated audience and make adjustments to the design accordingly. Also pay attention to differences in learning preferences. Some adults prefer to receive information visually; others, orally or verbally; others, kinesthetically (wanting to touch or experience in order to learn). Some adults need to do *all* three modes of taking in information to really learn something. So in the customer service training design, plan activities to accommodate the various styles of learning. You can be sure that the more senses you engage in the training/learning process, the greater the chance for learning to occur. This is called multisensory learning, which means to engage several senses in the delivery process.

The **training environment** is critical for a successful learning experience, especially for adults. Pay attention to the physical environment: the climate/room temperature, table arrangements, lighting, and refreshments.

It is hard to find a **climate or room temperature** that pleases all participants. You will need to find a middle-of-the-road temperature and stick with it, except for excesses in weather conditions. Remember that the size of your audience will also affect the temperature. Twenty-five people in a room will generate more heat than ten.

Be sure that the **room arrangement** reinforces what you want to accomplish. If you want a lot of interaction, do not use straight rows (theater style). Instead have tables, preferably round tables, grouped to minimize time spent in putting people into teams. Also, make sure that chairs are as comfortable as possible.

Lighting, or lack of, can be both a blessing and a challenge. If there are no windows, create a more open environment by placing colorful posters, quotations, or scenery on the walls. If there is too much light, arrange the seating so that the light will be a minimal distraction. If there are a lot of windows, you may need to arrange the participants so that their backs are to the windows; this will reduce outside distractions.

Believe it or not, the type of **refreshments** you serve can be seen as a plus or a minus in the end-of-class training evaluation. Participants *do* pay attention to what refreshments are served. Training budgets dictate how limited, or lavish, the refreshments will be. If you're going to serve a hot beverage like coffee, also offer tea. Always have ice water, and lots of it. If budget is not an issue, fresh fruit can be popular with the participants. Cookies are always a welcome treat and can fit into any budget, small or grand. By the way, if budget *is* an issue, and you conduct the customer service training with another department, you might be able to partner with that department and share the costs of the refreshments.

The psychological, or emotional, environment is as important as the physical one. A psychological environment is a place that is safe to discuss frustrations, issues, and concerns from the employees' point of view. These frustrations could be related to organizational/management practices (such as policies, procedures, or the lack of either) or other specific customer service challenges. It is important for the facilitator to ensure that it is okay to share such concerns, but the facilitator must temper the sharing of these concerns by supporting and respecting management. This is a fine line to which facilitators must be sensitive.

Be prepared to get your customer service training back on track should the conversation veer off toward a "gripe" session.

Using a Script

Do you want to use a script for your delivery? It's okay! How else would we remember what we were going to say if we didn't use a script? However, you'll need to practice. The most successful talent in the world rehearses and rehearses, over and over again.

To this day, whether I deliver one program a week, or five programs a week, I take time to go over my notes before *every* program no matter how many times I've delivered it in the past.

Here's a simple, but very important tip:

It's embarrassing to see a facilitator handling items and drop his notes only to pick them up out of order—not a very professional scene. You might want to punch a hole in the upper left corner of all the pages and put a steel ring through the hole so that the papers won't fall and get out of order.

I encourage you to *start* with a script. Add notes to it as time goes by.

Record Your Practice Presentation

Recording your presentation could be painful, but it's worth the effort. It's important for you to hear and see how you look and stand *before* you present to your audience. What are you doing with your hands? Your feet? Is your posture good? Are you smiling? Do you believe in what you're delivering? Even more important, does the audience believe what you're saying? You'll never know if you don't see or hear yourself in action.

There's no easy way to get good at delivering a program without practice, practice, and then *more practice.* While practice may or may not "make perfect," it will certainly ensure a higher level of comfort in terms of delivery. Ask someone whose opinion you value to critique your delivery.

 KEY POINT: If you're going to be standing in front of an audience holding a script, note cards, or anything with more than one page, remember this: number the pages and fasten them together at the top left corner.

Stage Fright

Does getting up in front of people make you nervous? You're not alone. Experts say it's the number two fear, second only to the fear of dying. Knowing that you're not alone won't fix the problem, but it may make you feel better.

There are plenty of first-time facilitators who feel uncomfortable standing up in front of a room full of people. While there are several books about the art of public speaking, I'm not sure reading these will fix stage fright.

My personal suggestion is to have several dry runs and rehearsals in front of those you trust, such as family, friends, or close coworkers, who will help you with this process.

You're going to need to rehearse anyway, so learn how to present better at the same time! Good luck!

TELEPHONE DOCTOR® CUSTOMER SERVICE TIP:	Relax! You *can* do it!

Selling the Training
to the Attendees:
Why Are They There?

Did you ever try to record a TV program on your DVD recorder and later find out you were on the wrong channel? What happened? You missed the program, right?

We have a similar circumstance in customer service training. It has to do with attitude. If the attendee's attitude is unreceptive, he or she is going to be on the wrong mental channel and miss the program. Often, that is the very person who needs the improvement the most.

You don't need a magic wand to clear up all the attitude problems you may face. Instead, try to draw the attendees out and move them toward being receptive toward customer service training. How do you do that? Humor is a big help. Here's one we sometimes use:

EXAMPLE: "How many of you don't want to be here today?"

Even if no hands go up, this question usually gets a chuckle, and laughter is a wonderful diffuser. It is extremely important to *acknowledge* the lack of interest and involvement. You already know going in that you may need to "sell" this customer service training to your audience.

Attendees' attitudes will vary from receptive to skeptical to downright hostile. We need to be aware of the attitudinal indicators of our attendees.

How can we tell? Here are some obvious hints:

You can start by observing body language. Watch for folded arms, slouching down in the seat, and a defiant facial expression. Also, notice if there's a lack of response to your engaging questions.

The reasons? Some attendees don't want to be there. Others will think they already know the material. A few resent authority. But the biggest and most often cited reason is that *they do not know why they are there.* The organization, or the manager, has not clearly communicated the need or the reason.

You can tell very early, and very easily, if they're glad to be there or not. If it's a group problem (and it frequently can be), you want *the group* to talk about how they're feeling about being there. Why are they so reluctant? There always will be someone who will speak up and tell you the real reason why they resent being there, because most of them have already discussed it. What you want to do is respond very carefully—not defend, not demand, not attack—but carefully *listen* to why they resent being there. Often when employees feel that they are being heard and know that you understand they didn't have a choice about attending, you can then negotiate with them to make the best of their involvement. You are being sensitive and understanding that "we're going to make this work."

EXAMPLE: You can tell the group:

> "A lot of things we'll talk about today you may already know . . . and the things that you do not know may give you a chance to see things differently."

If, on the other hand, it's an individual situation, with one or two people resisting, then you want to use the first break to talk privately with that person or persons about their resentment or lack of involvement.

CAUTION: When it comes to individuals, you don't want to assume that the lack of involvement is just an attitude problem. It may simply be a personality preference for introversion.

Another question that helps open up customer service training dialogue between the facilitator and the attendees (and can be asked and answered in a positive manner) is "How many of you think you already know how to give good customer service?"

Talk about the customer service process with the group. Mention that the company has identified some "best practices" in the organization and many of the attendees are the folks who are already doing that.

You can then come back with a soft appeal for an open mind like, "Why is customer service important?"

You can also ask the attendees to respond to your questions while in smaller groups. Divide the attendees into groups and have them report back within a limited amount of time. This gets them involved early on and makes it easier for introverts to participate, which, in turn, makes it easier for everyone to be involved and think out loud. It simplifies things if you acknowledge their "team" responses and answers instead of addressing them as a total group.

Another question that would be very important to ask, in either a large or small group, is "How many of you think you already give good service?"

The definition and class responses will allow you to open their minds for reinforcing or learning something new about customer service. What you're doing is building on what they already know. You can amplify that later in the content by talking about specific things relating to customer service and organizational values.

No one wants to act badly. Employees don't wake up in the morning and say, "I'm gonna make someone's day miserable." Things happen. Stuff happens. And how the situation is handled is the customer service you'll be talking about.

Discerning and addressing attitudes early in the customer service training program can make the class much more effective and meaningful for the individual as well as the rest of the attendees.

Activity:

To address an attitude of "I already know this," or "I already do customer service well," you might want to do a fun exercise that Bob Pike, president of Creative Techniques International, suggested. It takes about five minutes and will drive home the point that the attendees really don't know some things as well as they think they do.

Tell the class to do the following:

Up in the corner of a blank sheet of paper, ask each participant to write down the number of pennies they have handled in their lives. Have some or all (depending on group size) call out the figure they wrote down. Record these figures on a flip chart. Ask each to draw two large circles on the piece of paper. Ask them to refrain from taking a penny from their purse or pocket. Have them label one circle "front" and one "back." Ask them to reproduce the front and back of a penny in one minute. Point out how many they've handled. At the end of a minute, point out how we can be overly familiar with an object, situation, or event, and not really see it. Expand on this.

To learn the value of a team, ask each person to describe one thing they have on their drawing. As each gives a feature, the others add the feature to their drawings so that each picture becomes more and more complete through shared knowledge. Discuss the value of a team in an open forum.

Tell them they can now look at a penny. Allow time for them to do so and to comment to one another. Tell them the Treasury Department estimates we handle 1,000 pennies per year. Refer back to their estimates. Many will be over 100,000. Some may be over 1,000,000.

You may be asking, "Is it possible to turn an attitude around? Can I work with someone whose attitude is less than desirable and make her attitude better?" In most cases, yes, but it will take work on your part. It will take **coaching, encouragement, understanding,** and, most of all, **time** for customer service training. Most employees want to do a good job, but they have not been shown how. Be there for them.

If you need to promote customer service training within the office or building, put up strategically placed posters to let employees know in advance that customer service training is planned. Heighten their awareness. Advertise that there will be prizes, exercises, and a fun time for all.

Efforts to market training programs in customer service have proven their value time after time. Consider the possibility of putting together a basic sell job. It makes sense that such an endeavor would increase the attendees' enthusiasm and the payoff for the training.

 KEY POINT 1: We need to communicate to the attendees *why* they are there.

 KEY POINT 2: We need to be careful of how we judge a person's involvement when he or she is not participating.

Lecturing: Borrring!

Is lecturing boring? Maybe . . . maybe not.

A lecture is a formal, prepared presentation of information. The person talking is the center of attention. Simply put, that person introduces the subject, presents the information, and then summarizes the material. It is regarded largely as a passive (some would say boring) method of customer service training. The facilitator speaks, and the attendees listen and usually do not participate in any way.

As such, lectures have limitations. They can quickly become boring for attendees. Human nature makes it difficult to remain attentive to one person talking for any length of time. At least that seems to be true for most of us. Lecturing involves no feedback. There's no way of knowing if the attendees are really listening and learning. Are they getting the correct message of the lesson?

To get the greatest level of success with a training program, it is best to get attendees actively involved.

One approach can be called a "training conference." This technique combines or breaks up lectures with formal or programmed periods for questions and discussions. This obtains feedback and comprehension checks.

However, for all its drawbacks, the lecture format enables a facilitator to control the class (unless attendees fall asleep). This holds true especially with regard to the management of time. A sizable amount of content can be presented in the lecture method of lesson presentation.

As mentioned earlier, more information is retained and learned by seeing and doing than by passive listening. So even though you may be able to express a lot of information within the lecture format, the retention will not be there.

Straight lecture presentations without some type of interaction in customer service training usually are not effective.

Questions: How to Get Attendees Involved

Questions and questioning techniques can help improve the delivery of your customer service training. In particular, questions can be used to increase group discussion and attendee participation.

New facilitators often plan their lesson presentation primarily with statements and overlook the value of questions. Experienced facilitators use questions regularly. They know that questions can contribute in many ways to the effectiveness of a lesson. Questions can be used to

- find out relevant information;
- increase understanding of a training situation;
- elicit new ideas;
- correct misconceptions;
- demonstrate interest or concern;
- build relationships;
- encourage ownership; and
- build commitment.

There are various types of questions, but in customer service training, four types are most commonly used:

- Open-ended questions
- Closed-ended questions
- Probing questions
- Clarifying/restating questions

Open-Ended Questions

Open-ended questions cannot be answered in simple terms. They have, in reality, no fixed limit. They are intended to get attendees to open up and share details. They can give insight into the attendees' opinions and feelings. They stimulate continued conversation. They encourage attendees to talk, and they demonstrate that the facilitator wants to hear more.

EXAMPLES: "Can you tell me how you might approach this situation better next time?"

"Given the final result, what are your concerns about this way of dealing with an irate customer?"

Closed-Ended Questions

Closed-ended questions are often answered as "yes" or "no," or with a simple statement of fact. They let you get more *specific* information or highlight what the employee has said. They have a fixed limit, usually aiming for brief responses or to confirm facts. Good closed-ended questions encourage the attendee to provide information that you might want to supplement the lesson. Although they may be answered in only one or two words, closed-ended questions challenge the attendee to explore ideas, defend statements, and contribute to the discussion.

EXAMPLES: "Do you agree with this approach?"

"Is this the way you want to deal with this customer?"

Probing Questions

Probing questions may be either open-ended or closed-ended, and they result from listening to the attendee. They are follow-up questions that are asked in order to elicit more information. They encourage the conversation to continue by conveying to the employee that you are interested in what he or she is saying.

EXAMPLES: "What do you believe is the most difficult part of understanding customers?"

"How do you think this will work?"

Clarifying/Restating Questions

To clarify and restate, repeat in your own words the content of what the attendee has said. In other words, clarifying/restating questions clarify your statements.

EXAMPLES: "What I'm understanding you to say . . . "

"So what you're saying is . . . "

Good questioning techniques will help make the customer service training classes far more effective.

 KEY POINT: Involve the audience. Don't just lecture.

Problem Attendees: Every Class Has One (At Least!)

As we all might know, there's a common major irritation in customer service training: **difficult attendees.** As mentioned earlier, some attendees are reluctant or fearful of change or of having to master something new. Some feel they know it all already, while others don't want to be there for any number of reasons.

The first requisite in dealing with problem attendees is to *accept* the fact that they exist. The second is to *avoid* becoming defensive. The third is to *resolve* to take appropriate steps to deal with resistance.

Who are some of the most common problem participants? Well, let's talk about some of the ones who have irritated us most through the years.

The Controller

The controller is the attendee who must dominate the discussion, which is okay once in a while, but not always. To deal with overbearing attendees, the facilitator can attempt to summarize their views in an effort to end the comments. The facilitator can also divert them by asking them to take notes. It's difficult to take notes and talk at the same time— try it yourself! Or call upon other attendees for their views. Sometimes it's necessary during breaks or at the end of a class to talk to the controller attendee. Suggest strongly that while his or her input is valued, other attendees need to have an opportunity to contribute.

The Challenger

Another problem attendee, a variant of the talkative attendee, is the one who disagrees with just about everything. Challengers will not accept any other view but their own. They can become highly critical of other facilitators and other attendees and even be sarcastic. This conduct cannot, of course, be tolerated. Often the group may make an effort to control the situation. A stern warning by the facilitator could be necessary. The challenger is frustrating because he or she will be taking up time that is better used for training. While we've heard of cases in which such a problem attendee was not invited back to the class, that's not the answer to one who challenges every technique or subject matter.

A private conversation with this individual is suggested so that you can find out his or her *real* objection to being at the class. Challenging or arguing can be a smoke screen for something else.

The Distracter

The distracter is less harmful to the integrity of the lesson than the previous two. However, this person also can be a problem. Often, unknowingly, distracters tend to lead the discussion in directions other than those planned for the lesson. They can get sidetracked into personal situations that are far afield of the topics that should be considered. The anecdotes are often interesting and even amusing, but don't contribute to the content. While some of these folks mean well, it can become a nuisance. The facilitator should mention to them that their ideas are interesting and to "hold that thought" because they are going to move on and talk about the next topic.

"Hold that thought" is a great way to move on to another subject.

Most veteran facilitators can cite various types of problem attendees who have irked them in the past. Again, these people exist and must be managed.

 KEY POINT: Deal with these problem attendees gently but firmly.

Rewards: Prizes and Motivation Dramatically Increase Participation

There's a saying in customer service training: "Catch 'em doing something right and then reward them!"

Adults, just like kids, like rewards: candy and small gimmicks are often much-sought-after participation rewards. Use them to your advantage.

Open praising, while embarrassing to some, is an ego booster, and most attendees enjoy the spotlight.

Think about ways you can give positive feedback in your customer service training. Here are a few ideas we've used in the classroom setting:

- Dots on the back of booklets or bottom of chairs for random prizes.

- "Let's Make A Deal"
  If the employee has, let's say, a library card with them, we give them a reward. Or you can ask for a 1942 penny and then give them a reward. It's a feel-good game and that's worth a lot.

- Offer prizes that correlate to the training segment, such as:
  — A mirror for their desk to remind them to smile
  — Buttons that say "I'm good"
  — "YES, I CAN" buttons

I saw a button at one of my clients' offices that said, "The answer is Yes. Now what is the question?" The button made me feel very good.

Rewarding early participation can dramatically increase class participation.

But performance appraisal is the best reward you can give employees. Put it in writing. Let them know you put a good note about them in their employee file.

Finishing with a Flourish: Your Time to Shine

After a little experience as a facilitator, you'll have a sense of how to time your customer service presentation content so that it lasts until the end of the lesson. You'll have a feel for what should be discussed at various points during the hour or two (or whatever time period) for this training. You'll know when to pick up the pace and when you can consider a point in greater depth so that the conclusion of the content is reached when the lesson is scheduled to end.

A special effort should be made to build up to a climax at the end of the class. The most important ideas, or "key concepts," should be summarized, expanded, and emphasized. In other words, when the people leave, it should be with the most important thoughts that were presented during the lesson in mind.

EXAMPLE: In a basic course on customer communications, the lesson on listening might stress the difference between hearing and listening. This difference needs to be remembered in talking to customers. So ask attendees a question or two about this and then build your final thoughts on these answers:

"Remember, as we saw demonstrated today, hearing is one thing. Listening is another. There's a big difference between hearing and being a good listener. So don't just hear your customers—truly listen to them! Thank you for your time today. I enjoyed it."

Or consider the steps involved in dealing with an irate customer. Stress the need to pause for just a moment in the discussion to regain professional composure.

Or emphasize the need for customer service representatives to remember that the customer is not angry with them, but at the situation. And to remember why they are on the receiving end of the irritation. And so on.

It's a great feeling to have an attendee come up and tell you, "That was great, thanks." That's finishing with a flourish!

TELEPHONE DOCTOR® CUSTOMER SERVICE TIP:	It doesn't hurt to end a few minutes early!

 KEY POINT: Quite simply, make the final moments of your class memorable, and thank the attendees for participating.

Evaluation
Component

Evaluation: How'd Ya Do?

Evaluation is the fourth part of the process needed to develop customer service training. Evaluation can be defined as examining, or judging carefully, the value of something— in this case, the success of your training.

We can evaluate how attendees liked a single class, or we can evaluate how well the attendees *understood* the material. We also can evaluate employee performance to determine behavior change. Additionally, we can evaluate the training program from the point of view of the customer and ask "Has their satisfaction increased?"

All of these evaluations are important, and, in each case, there is more than one way to conduct the evaluation.

The primary purpose of evaluation is to determine whether the customer service training outcomes were achieved. It's very simple:

- Was the program well organized and complete with relevant information?
- Did the attendees learn what they were supposed to learn?
- Are there improvements in their behavior?
- Is this training helping improve customer service?
- Is there great customer satisfaction?

Evaluation can be effective both during the customer service program and at its conclusion. It is frequently an ongoing process of observing improvements in behavior and customer satisfaction over a sustained period of time.

Evaluations may be conducted by the facilitator during the class to assess progress or may be conducted after the class to assess the class itself. The evaluation of improved performance and customer satisfaction is commonly conducted by supervisors and team leaders or other departments.

Some organizations believe this evaluation aspect is so important that they have entire departments whose sole purpose is to assess and evaluate all elements of customer/representative interaction, and some even tie the results to a paycheck.

 KEY POINT: Realize that evaluation is only one element of a successful customer service training program.

Classroom Evaluations: The Verdict Is In

At the end of a training class, attendees are often asked to evaluate the class itself. A valid evaluation will indicate ways in which the course could be improved and how the facilitator might be more effective. This information can provide direction for the facilitator to adapt the customer service training program in the future.

There are a number of ways to evaluate customer service training.

Evaluation sheets can be created or adapted from previous training courses or from sheets supplied with off-the-shelf programs. Written evaluations are the most commonly used. The questions can be put forth in different formats:

- True or false
- Multiple choice
- Fill-in-the-blank
- Match-up
- Essays
- Checklists
- Any combination of the above

In creating your evaluation form, consider these questions to guide you in formulating questions:

- What was your intended outcome?
- What did you plan/hope to accomplish with the training?
- How did the participants react to the training activities?
- How did the participants react to your training style?

Ask questions that will give you the desired information. Open-ended questions such as "What did you like best?" and "How will you use the information you learned?" are valuable, but require more time and thought than a structured checklist. Attendees often don't want to take the time to fill out a long form.

A combination of checklist and open-ended questions provides a good format for comments. Here are two examples of classroom evaluations using both checklist and open-ended questions.

Sample 1
Standard Evaluation Form

Course Title: _____ Date:_____

Location:_____

Instructor: _____

To guide us in planning future seminars and workshops, please answer the questions below. You need not sign the sheet unless you want to.

How would you rate the following?

	Excellent	Satisfactory	Unsatisfactory
Quality of Presentation			
Adequacy of Course Content			
Length of Course			
Adequacy of Course Materials			
Conduct of Workshops			
Adequacy of Facilities			

(continued)

Sample 1: Standard Evaluation Form *(concluded)*

If any factor is rated "Unsatisfactory," please explain:

_____

_____

What was of the most value to you in this seminar?

_____

_____

What was of the least value to you in this seminar?

_____

_____

Additional comments would be appreciated!

_____

_____

This page may be reproduced for use in a
customer service training program.

Sample 2
Training Evaluation Form

Thank you for attending our workshop today. Please take a minute to let us know how well today's training met your needs.

1. Please rate the following: 1–5   (5 being best)

    This workshop was useful.   _____

    I enjoyed the workshop.   _____

    The material related to my job.   _____

    Topics were clear and easy to understand.   _____

    I will use these skills.   _____

    Our company needs more training like this.   _____

    Please rate the instructor.   _____

2. Overall rating for this workshop.   _____

3. Would you recommend this class to coworkers?   _____

4. Would you recommend this class to your manager?   _____

(continued)

Sample 2: Training Evaluation Form *(concluded)*

5. What did you learn today that would help you be more effective on the job?

_____

_____

_____

6. What areas could we change to improve this class?

_____

_____

_____

Signed: _____ Date:_____

A simple verbal question such as "How did you react to this training session?" will give you some feedback.

Even a "smile" sheet, where attendees make a smile face or a frown face as an evaluation of whether they got something out of the class, may be appropriate if you will never repeat the training or if you have no option to change anything.

Evaluations in most cases are a necessary evil: necessary because you find out how a program was accepted and what the attendees learned and evil, sometimes, because they give an opportunity to those who may resent the customer service training to attack either the facilitator or the training (responses may range from "It was too cold in the room" to "The facilitator's outfit distracted me"). This is why, if you are going to put an evaluation sheet in front of attendees, it's best you put on your suit of armor because now it's their turn to teach you a few things. Expect it.

Secondhand feedback on evaluations is also important. An attendee may say one thing in class to you face-to-face, yet may share a negative comment with his or her supervisor. A comment of this nature needs to be followed up because it can render your customer service training ineffective and can be dangerous to your overall training.

However, when secondhand feedback is positive, evaluation of your training becomes more believable, credible, and emotionally supportive.

For the most part, when the training works and your delivery was good, you'll get the biggest thrill when the attendee fills out the comment section with, "Thank you! I really learned a lot and will put it all to use."

When your customer service training receives high marks, that's great ammunition for future programs to management and even to expand the budget for the next time.

 KEY POINT 1: The format of the evaluation isn't as important as doing one.

 KEY POINT 2: Positive secondhand feedback on evaluations is important.

Testing:
What Do They Know?
What Did They Learn?

Testing is one of the ways to evaluate training success. Some facilitators always test, while others never test. There is no specific "right" way.

Pretests can be done at the beginning of the class. You may even want to distribute them before the class as a teaser of what's coming.

Inventorying skills prior to training will allow you to assess the level of improvement after the training is complete. During your customer service training, testing will provide feedback on the progress of the attendees, or lack of it, so that any training problems can be identified before the lessons move on and the point is lost.

Separate evaluations can be given for each major topic in the course lessons. This will allow facilitators to correct mistakes, give positive feedback, and reinforce the new skill.

There are many effective methods to test the ongoing accomplishment of training:

- **True/false written tests** are quick to complete and grade. They can accurately reflect the level of achievement.

- **Discussion evaluation** is when the facilitator asks questions that draw out responses. Each of the questions must be carefully devised and skillfully presented. The purpose is to initiate and sustain a lively dialogue that detects how much the attendees have learned.

- **Group assignments** offer a viable option in the area of customer service training. In this approach, the facilitator creates a real-life scenario that requires attendees to apply a concept discussed in the training. These mini-case studies require a decision to be made or a problem to be solved. Each attendee could individually outline a course of action, and then the group could discuss the various alternatives as well as the pros and cons associated with them.

- **Posttests** can be done at the completion of the class. They can be done open-book or from memory. When compared to pretest responses, the posttest results can provide documentation of training success.

Whatever testing methods you choose to include, a poor test response by a number of attendees could signify possible adjustments that can be made in content, instructional materials, or delivery.

If attendees do not understand the principles, re-evaluate:

- Is the material off target?
- Is the method of instruction inappropriate?
- Are the tests defective?
- Have supervisors failed to endorse or reinforce the importance of the training?

Behavior Change: Can Old Dogs Learn New Tricks?

A well-designed customer service training program includes many elements that encourage attendees to change their current behaviors to be more customer service friendly. Some of these elements include the following:

- Clearly stated customer service training objectives
- Well-organized, relevant content
- Opportunities for skill practice and role play in the classroom
- Verbal feedback to reinforce new skills and correct misconceptions
- Handout material, or "cheat sheets," as reminders of the new skills

After the course is concluded, surveillance or monitoring of attendees for improved skills and enhanced behavioral patterns in customer service is recommended. After all, the training goal is to impart new skills that actually change behavior.

The key is learning if the attendees are applying what was presented in the course as they work with customers.

Evaluating what behavior has changed is sometimes the responsibility of the facilitator, but is often also the responsibility of supervisors or team leaders. Whoever evaluates must be aware of the skills taught and be on the lookout for behavior change that represents mastery of the new customer service skills. Evaluation can be done in a casual "walking around the department" method (observing someone doing something right and letting him or her know). It is a valuable way to reinforce behavior change. A gold star, a pat on the back, a written or verbal commendation: all can reinforce the new skills learned.

A formal monitoring, or mystery-shopping, process also may be implemented. In a face-to-face service method, attendees are observed for their personal communications, for their efficiency in helping customers, and for their cordiality. On the telephone, monitoring attendees for their efficiency, friendliness, and, in particular, their verbal mannerisms, can provide valuable evaluation.

Formal evaluation requires the development of a "report card" to use during the evaluation. This report card should be specific and tied closely to the skills imparted in the customer service training class.

A point system may be beneficial when you use the report card. Award or deduct points for certain behaviors. Create charts and graphs from the combined results.

The most important element of following up is that the results are shared. Monitoring, or mystery shopping, done to provide only numerical data does little to reinforce customer service training effort. Management should hear of successes as well as failures. Attendees should be complimented for improved behavior and corrected for behavior that has not improved. Customer service training should be developed to address deficiencies that are universal.

 KEY POINT: Essentially, has the performance gap been eliminated or at least narrowed?

Why Your Training Didn't Work

by David Friedman, Vice President, General Manager, Telephone Doctor®

Every once in awhile, a client will tell us something like this: "Your training program was excellent! We could immediately see a big improvement, but after awhile, they seemed to go back to their old ways."

You may have encountered this phenomenon yourself. The answer to this puzzle lies in the fact that training only deals with improving skills. There are plenty of times when performance is poor, yet a lack of skills isn't the real problem.

Here are a few things the Telephone Doctor® believes may be sabotaging your training efforts:

1. **Not communicating expectations:** Have you clearly communicated the message that delivering a high level of service is a mandatory part of the employee's position? That you simply won't accept anything less?

2. **Lack of consequences for not reaching expectations:** Do you have a quantitative or qualitative method to measure whether the employee is performing up to your standards? What are the ramifications if he or she doesn't?

3. **Lack of management buy-in:** Management *must* speak the same language as employees. If superior customer service is truly important, then front-line staff needs to see management taking things seriously, too. Don't send mixed messages.

4. **Operational or technological gap:** If you're asking one switchboard attendant to handle 3,000 calls per day, it's far fetched to expect him or her to treat each caller with attentive personal service.

The test for determining whether you have a "skills" problem is to learn the answer to the question: "After training, could they perform up to your standards if they were forced to?"

If the answer is "No," then you've still got a training problem.

If the answer is "Yes, but . . .," don't blame training. You have other issues to address.

Other Considerations

It Should Never Take Two People to Deliver Good Customer Service

This chapter illustrates that *it should never take two people to deliver good customer service.* Read on.

When Telephone Doctor® went looking for the "world's worst customer service story," we received over 1,200 letters, faxes, e-mails, and other stories.

After reading them, we selected what we felt were the best— or shall we say the worst—and then gave them the "how it should have been done" treatment. We compiled the results in a book that has become a great training tool, especially for smaller staffed offices and departments. There's barely an industry that isn't included, and the reader will recognize at least a few situations.

The winning story proves our theory: It should never take two people to give good customer service. Here's the letter:

> En route to another state to visit my terminally ill mother, I stopped along the roadside to call and check on her condition. I discovered I had forgotten my phone credit card and asked the operator to charge the call to my home number. The operator told me that someone had to be at my house to approve the charge.
>
> I explained that there was no one there and that the call was a seriously important one. After a long silence (I thought I had been disconnected), I said, "Hello?" The operator finally replied nastily, "What part of the word *no* can't you understand?"

I then asked to speak to the operator's supervisor. After a lengthy wait, the supervisor came on the line, listened to my plight, and helpfully found a way to make the call. The supervisor then indicated she would reconnect me to the operator who would complete the call. After another long wait, I again said, "Hello?" and the original operator—I recognized her curt voice—demanded an apology.

When the call was finally put through, I learned from my father that my mother had died a few minutes before.

Apart from the heart-wrenching human tragedy of the incident, this experience demonstrates customer service at its world class worst.

First, no customer should ever have to endure such rude, abrasive treatment. Second, in an emergency, a policy should be in place to adapt, or waive, the rules to accommodate the caller. Third, and most important, it should never require a second person to give good customer service. **You need to empower your staff**.

In this unfortunate case, the operator had a wonderful opportunity to give great customer service—and lost it. Contrary to all customer service rules, one inept and uncivil service person, the bad apple in the cart, turned an opportunity for great customer service into a totally unnecessary, crushing incident.

One of the ways you can start off in a customer service training class is to have the audience think of the times they've had their own "customer service nightmares" and discuss them in detail. Make sure you write down the good points. Then in discussing with your group how it *should have* been done, try to recreate the nightmare as it might happen at your place of business. The more you can customize a problem to your business, the easier it becomes to solve the problem.

In delivering your customer service training, remember that the more "empowerment" you can give your employees when they are working with a customer, the better customer service your company will give.

Employees enjoy the feeling of being able to say "Yes" to a customer. Work with management to find out exactly how much empowerment your employees can have when working with a customer. It may be a dollar amount, a product they are allowed to "bonus" in, or whatever your company will allow. You will find a better sense of ownership for the problem when employees are allowed to make a decision.

Worried that they'll make the wrong decision or go too far? That's what guidelines are for. I doubt an employee would give the store away. Let them know how far they can go and when the customer needs to be directed to a supervisor.

Customers very much dislike going from employee to employee when they have a a problem, a concern, or simply a question. I would venture to say 80 percent of all situations that come into your organization could be handled easily by your employees, if you give them the opportunity to learn how to do it.

 KEY POINT: It *never* should take two people to deliver good customer service.

Band-Aid® Training

Band-Aid training is pretty much what it sounds like. What happens when you slice your finger down to the bone and it bleeds and bleeds and bleeds? You probably want to run to the emergency room for stitches. What would have happened if you put a bandage on that deep cut instead of going to the hospital? It might not have healed properly, would it? And if it bled badly enough, more bad things could have happened such as infection.

Band-Aid training is similar. Let's say you receive one or two complaint letters about a product—or worse—about an employee who represents you and your company. You think to yourself, one or two complaint letters about "Mary," who has been with you three years and has never had a complaint on her record—well, that's not too bad. And yet, as an owner or a manager, you do recognize it must be attended to.

"Mary," you say, "you've been here three years and have done a super job. Unfortunately, we've received a couple complaints about your service, so I'd like you to be more careful. In fact, I think it would be good for you to watch one of those customer service training DVDs we ordered a while back."

"Sure," she replies. And Mary does. She takes an hour break and watches one or two DVDs and then she comes back to work.

You've just put a "bandage" on something that needed "emergency room treatment." Just like a deep cut is not going to heal properly if you just put a bandage on it, behavior isn't going to change by watching one DVD, reading one book, or being spoken to by the boss one time. Repetition is the mother of learning.

Mary needed to "get to the emergency room." She needed customer service training that would help make sure she *understood* what she did to upset the customer. Moreover she needed to realize *how* it could have been prevented, and more importantly, how to make sure it never happened again.

The perception of the customer, be it on a product or an employee, is all that counts. Perception is *everything*.

Band-Aid training isn't terrible. A lot of companies do it. But, in truth, we know it isn't going to make the permanent change we need. It may help for a week, a month, maybe even three months, but then the bandage comes off, just like on the cut, and you still have the scar tissue that didn't heal properly—the person receiving Band-Aid training didn't make the behavior change properly.

In effect, Band-Aid training is "short-term" training. And that's not what you want for your organization. You want changes that will be permanent—customer service training that will make a difference. If you select Band-Aid training, then "get to an emergency room" shortly thereafter.

When you're doing Band-Aid training, at least be sure you're treating the right problem.

EXAMPLE: If Mary's problem was job knowledge, there's no value in showing her a DVD on saying "please" and "thank you."

You'll need to find out exactly what happened. What we need to understand is that when we recreate a scene with a customer, it is seldom as it happened. Often words are changed, and the tone of voice is different. That's why it's important to get to the problem area as soon as it happens. Our memories, along with the customer's, fade all too soon on these things, and we don't always get the story right.

EXAMPLE: I had an experience at a large department store a while back. The salesclerk was totally uninterested in wrapping a gift for me. My husband and I seldom report people. Nevertheless, this time I felt the need to go the general manager of this large chain department store. When I told him my story, he promptly told me, "As soon as I get the story from the salesclerk, I'll call you." I stared in disbelief. It was as though he didn't believe me and wanted to get the "right story" from his employee. How do you think I felt? Not very good. It's taken me years to give that store any further business.

TELEPHONE DOCTOR® CUSTOMER SERVICE TIP:	No matter what you think, no matter how you feel, no matter if the customer is wrong (and sometimes he or she is), it is paramount to let customers know that you value comments and thank them for coming to you.

 KEY POINT: Bottom line: Band-Aid training doesn't treat the root of the problem.

Customer Service Training Topics

There are an unlimited number of customer service topics to be considered for inclusion in your training. Here are some of the more important customer service training topics you should not miss. Keep them in mind when you design your classes.

- Handling irate customers
- Putting callers on hold
- Building rapport with customers
- Taking messages
- Welcoming the customer
- Smiling
- Maximizing voice mail
- Improving your tone of voice
- Listening skills
- Dealing with internal customers
- Interpreting foreign accents

What topics can you add?

Us in *Customer*

As you can see, there is no "I" in the word *customer.*
Customer service means "team." It involves all of us.
This golden rule will apply in customer service forever.
Train your employees to go that extra step every time.
Ask one more question to be sure the customer is satisfied.

Can we satisfy every customer every time? Probably not. But,
like the famous Mark Twain adage, if "you can please most
of the people most of the time," you're doing great. There
will always be people who are miserable and unhappy about
everything, no matter *how* good you make it for them. That's
unfortunate.

Summary

Bottom line (pun intended!), providing good customer service is essential to the success of any organization. If your customers are happy, they will be loyal customers and refer others.

This book covered quite a bit of material, but it is all common sense. With the components provided, you are now empowered to create your own customer service training program and make it as basic or as elaborate as you choose.

- Analyze/assess the needs of your customers.
- Get top management to buy in to the need for training.
- Promote the training classes to the employees as a fun way to improve customer service.
- Determine those individuals in your organization who should receive training.
- Determine what information those individuals need to know, and plan your classes accordingly.
- Include lots of visuals, handouts, audio, role playing, prizes, and rewards.
- Get feedback from your attendees' evaluations of your delivery.
- Provide ongoing opportunities to reinforce what you taught them.
- Be prepared to receive compliments for a job well done!

Potpourri

This is like the P.S. in a letter. It includes things we wanted to share with you in other chapters but, for one reason or another, didn't fit or that we forgot. These are miscellaneous items that will help make your customer service training smoother *and* make the difference.

For instance, nowhere in the book could I find a spot to tell you about some of the various organizations that specialize in customer service. You're able to join these organizations and reap many benefits from them.

ICSA

International Customer Service Association. Sounds perfect, huh? Well, it *is* a good organization. You can find all sorts of information by calling (312) 321-6800 or writing to ICSA, 401 North Michigan Avenue, Chicago, IL 60611. Visit their Web site at www.icsa.org.

SOCAP

Society of Consumer Affairs Professionals. Find out more by calling (703) 519-3700 or write them at SOCAP, 801 North Fairfax Street, Suite 404, Alexandria, VA 22314, or visit SOCAP's Web site at www.socap.org.

ASTD

American Society of Training and Development. This is the premier organization for the human resource industry. If you are already a member, then you are aware of the value of this fine organization. There's an enormous amount of invaluable information available from ASTD. The phone number is (703) 683-8100 or write them at ASTD, 1640 King Street, Alexandria, VA 22313. Visit their Web site at www.astd.org.

ASTD has local chapters in some cities, as does ICSA and SOCAP. You can join a local chapter and, if it fits your needs, join the national chapter. Local chapters usually have monthly meetings and bring in speakers who will provide you with additional information. If you're having difficulty finding a local chapter for any organization, call the national office and ask if it has a local chapter nearby. The benefit of the local chapters is that you will meet other people with the same job position or duties as you. You will have stories to share, and you can learn a lot about how other companies are putting together the same type of information you are. Peer groups are great!

HDI Help Desk International

With 7,500 members worldwide, HDI is the largest association for IT service and support professionals. As such, HDI produces numerous publications, hosts several symposiums and two conferences each year, and certifies hundreds of help desk and service desk professionals each month. Visit HDI's Web site for full information: www.thinkhdi.com. The phone number is (800) 248-5667. The address is 102 South Tejon, Suite 1200, Colorado Springs, CO 80803.

Other Useful Information

Each of the national organizations has an annual conference with an agenda and, in most cases, exhibitors as well as local monthly chapter meetings. The exhibitors will provide you with an abundance of training material on virtually any topic and a vast array on customer service training. There's simply so much information out there. With new technology, you can usually get exactly what you want, in any format you prefer: DVDs, books, CDs, Internet, audio, and more.

As one might suspect, each of the organizations has a monthly or quarterly magazine, newsletter, or report of some type for its members. These periodicals will also provide information you'll be able to use in developing your customer service training.

There may be circumstances when you won't have time to do a customer service training class, or the analysis, let alone the design.

There are other ways you can get the customer service information to your employees. They may not be in the "formal" classroom method you like or had hoped for, but they will work, and that's the important thing.

Brown Bag Lunches

Many companies have used this method very successfully. Bring your employees together during a lunch period and spend that hour talking about customer service. Perhaps show a customer service DVD or listen to an audiotape. You could even have the participants talk about what kind of morning they had as it pertains to the customers.

About the Author

Interviews, Articles, and Books

Nancy Friedman is a frequent guest on top television and radio talk shows (*Oprah, Today Show, CBS This Morning, Good Morning America,* CNN, WOR, WGN, KMOX, FOX News, VCCO, KCMO, to name a few).

She is the author of hundreds of articles in leading newspapers and magazines, including "Manager's Journal" in the *Wall Street Journal* and *USA Today.* Nancy is also the author of six best-selling books on customer service and communication skills.

Presentations and Awards

Nancy is one of America's most "asked back" speakers to conferences such as the insurance industry's Million Dollar Round Table; Professional Conference Managers Association; National Association of Mortgage Brokers; International Health, Racquet & Sportsclub Association, and the Air Conditioning Contractors of America, just to mention a few.

She has appeared on programs with such giants as General Colin Powell, Ken Blanchard, Bobby Knight, and Lou Holtz, and she was a featured speaker at the Tom Hopkins Sales Boot Camp. It is a perfect fit for owners, managers, top-level executives, and sales departments.

In addition, chambers of commerce from across the country have brought in Nancy to provide customer service, value-added programs for their own members and staff.

Nancy was selected as one of the 25 Most Influential Business Women in St. Louis. An avid Johnny Cash fan, Nancy promises she won't sing at her programs, but she will give you information you'll be able to use immediately.

Personal Information

Born and raised in Chicago, Illinois, Nancy and her husband, Dick, who travels with her, have owned two radio stations in San Diego and St. Louis. They have been working together for so many years that when asked, "How do you do that?" their answer is, "We've been doing it so long, we didn't know it shouldn't work." The Friedmans and their family live in West County, St. Louis, Missouri.

Other Books by Nancy Friedman, The Telephone Doctor®

Telephone Skill from A to Z

Telesales Tips from A to Z

Customer Service Nightmares

50 Little Tips that Make a Big Difference

The Good the Bad and the Ugly

How to Contact
Nancy Friedman,
The Telephone Doctor®

Telephone Doctor® means results. Over 22,000 clients include training professionals, human resource personnel, customer service managers, sales managers, and businesspersons who share a desire to help their business grow by providing world-class customer service.

In just over 20 years, Telephone Doctor® Customer Service Training has become a familiar and valued brand name within corporate training and development departments. Over half of the company's current business is the result of repeat or referrals. Core offerings continue to be the Complete Customer Service Training Library and on-site instructor-led workshops. Telephone Doctor® also offers keynote presentations, a comprehensive e-learning platform, as well as a growing series of business animations.

The next time you're frustrated by poor service you receive, remember that there are dozens of staff members and thousands of their customers who are glad that a poorly handled phone call back in 1982 resulted in this very unique company!

Telephone Doctor®
30 Hollenberg Court
St. Louis, Missouri, USA 63044
(314) 291-1012 Voice
(314) 291-3710 FAX
Web site: www.telephonedoctor.com
e-mail: info@telephonedoctor.com

153